Low-Budget Vegetarian Cooking

Eating Well in Challenging Times

Charles Obert

Revised and Expanded Edition

Published and printed in the United States of America

ISBN-13: 978-0-9864187-6-1

https://lowbudgetvegetarian.com

Dedication

To my daughter **Eve Obert**. The first edition of this book was written when Eve was in college. I wanted to share some simple tips about vegetarian cooking so she could continue to enjoy it. Apparently it worked, as she is now a very fine vegetarian cook in her own right, which is quite a challenge considering she has two grade-school age daughters.

And, to **Beverly White**. Back when I was at Macalester College in the early 1970's Beverly published a little spiral bound cookbook named, *Living High on the Bean*. That is the book that got me started on the style of vegetarian cooking I still use today. (Fortunately that was before I found out that it was stylish to look down on rice and beans with disdain as food for the poor and uneducated.) I think of my little cookbook as being a kind of sequel to her book.

"Red beans and ricely yours."

- Louis Armstrong

Table of Contents

New Preface - 2021

I originally wrote and released the first version of this cookbook online back in 2005. Obviously, a lot has changed since then.

As I mention in the original preface which follows this, the purpose of this book is to give you the skills to shop for and cook hearty, satisifying and nutritious meals using grains, beans and vegetables. If you buy unprocessed foods and learn how to prepare them yourself, these are easily the most useful and economical food investment you can make. The cooking techniques and suggestions can be adapted to the foods that are most readily available to you.

This is particularly important right at this point in time. As I write this, Summer 2021 in the United States, it appears that the economy is very unstable. I have already noticed that food prices have been going up in the past year, and I expect that to continue and perhaps accelerate in the future. Food and other supply shortages also seem like a definite possibility.

It really helps to know how to shop low on the food chain, cook simply, and still eat well and live well. This is an economical skill that may be becoming a survival skill.

I have kept the text and recipes of the original book mostly the same. I removed some recipes using ingredients that have now become hard to find or too expensive. I have also added some new recipes that have become favorites for me over the years.

At the end of the original text I have added an essay talking about how my shopping and cooking has changed since the first edition. Basically, I have taken my simple cooking style and made it even simpler. I also give some ideas about simple cooking for one based on my experience living alone for the past 12 years.

Changing our Attitude Towards Food

If I am right that we are heading for some challenging and unstable times, then I think it is worth taking a moment to think about our attitude towards food and eating.

If I look at how food and eating is presented in the media - on cooking sites, on dieting sites, and in advertisement and marketing - the following themes show up a lot.

Food as status signaling - eating the latest trendy new food, the one that Everyone Else is eating. Equally important is avoiding being seen eating low-brow, common foods - like, say, beans and rice.

Food as a luxury of the affluent - this ties in with the status signaling. If you look at the different trendy diets, you will routinely see foods recommended that are pricey enough to be out of the range of lower class working people. The Paleo diet is a good example - all fresh, all organic, grass fed premium beef, only wild caught and fresh fish and so on. That gets very expensive very quickly.

And, most important -

Food as Entertainment - Eating needs to be Fun. The worst thing you could say about food is that it is Plain or Boring.

This lets us be Picky Eaters, and I think we are trained to be picky as we grow up. I know I was, and I suspect most young people now are being taught that.

In our coming challenging world we need to get back to something very basic.

We eat to nourish ourselves and to stay alive.

That means being thankful for what we can afford, or what is available. It means eating plain common foods and being thankful. Eat what is available or go without. I think it may take some serious hard times before most of us can sit down to a plate of simple rice, beans and vegetables, and be really grateful that we have it.

Hopefully we are coming to a place where the thought of dumping the better part of a plate of food into the trash because a Picky Eater didn't want to touch it will seem like an obscene and wasteful act of gross ingratitude.

For picky eaters of all ages, sometimes the best answer to someone saying, I don't like this and I don't want to eat it, is simply - This is what we have; eat this or go hungry. That is a life lesson well worth learning.

This is what we have;

be grateful that we have it, give thanks,

and treat it like the precious gift it is.

Preface - Please Read This First

I want to talk about what I am trying to do with this little book, and how to get the most out of it. This is to encourage you to read and use all of the book, and to resist the temptation to skip over the first part of the book to get at the recipes.

There seems to be a prevailing popular myth in our culture that eating a diet with little or no meat or dairy products is difficult, or boring, or expensive, and that it takes a lot more time and effort to 'replace' animal food in a healthy diet.

I find the opposite to be true, and this book is written to give you the basic knowledge and tools you need to have a diet that is primarily or completely based on grains, vegetables and beans, that is nutritious, interesting, and inexpensive, and that takes no more cooking effort that you would need for a healthy meat-based diet.

Grains, vegetables and beans, taken together, make up the core of the traditional diets of most people around the world for most of our history on our planet. They are the core foods that I talk about preparing in this book.

For those of you who have concerns about digestibility of beans, I have an extensive section on making beans easy to digest, in which I pull together cooking techniques and digestive aid spices from different cuisines.

This cookbook is not intended primarily as a collection of recipes. It is designed to teach you how to naturally think and cook like a low budget vegetarian. In our culture especially, I find that most people have a hard time thinking of planning meals that aren't built around a meat dish. So, people who are new to vegetarian cooking often think in terms of replacing the meat, rather than thinking of how to use grains, beans and vegetables for what they do well in their own right.

I will cover the following main topics -

• how to buy these main foods in a way that is inexpensive but still gives you good quality food

• how to cook and combine these foods in such a way that they are interesting, tasty and easily digestible

• proportions of foods that make for a balanced and satisfying eating experience

• separate chapters on cooking grains, on beans and peas, and on salads

• how to cook ahead while still varying foods so you can deal with lunches and preparing workday meals ahead of time

• how to use a few basic spice patterns to vary taste as much as you please.

Opening Section

The opening sections of this book cover the basic skills of meal planning, shopping and cooking that you will need. They are intended to give you basic ways to prepare grains, vegetables and beans that apply to a wide variety of recipes.

Spice Patterns

The section on spice patterns is one of the most important and useful parts of the book. These are different combinations of spices that go well together. This provides a framework you can use to improvise and create your own recipes with confidence. I have organized them around the most common spices used in different vegetarian traditions from around the world, including Indian, Middle Eastern and Mexican. Once you get a handle on these, you can take the same basic grains and vegetables, and cook and Indian style meal one night, and a Mexican meal the next.

Master these patterns and you will never, ever get tired of cooking with grains, beans and vegetables.

In each of the sections on spice patterns I include a list of the recipes that use that particular pattern, so you can learn by example.

*** Recipe Patterns or Templates ***

This is the core of the book. Whatever you look at in the first part of the book, please be sure to carefully read this section.

If you use many cookbooks at all - which I have, over the past 50 plus years - you will start to notice that even cookbooks that look like they have hundreds of recipes, actually have only a handful of recipe patterns, with some variants on the ingredients. Once you really understand a recipe pattern, you have the ability to take similar ingredients and come up with your own individual variants, your own recipes. Do enough cooking and you will develop your own personal cook's instinct, that guides you to what mix of ingredients and spices feels right for this particular meal. That's where you start really being a vegetarian cook.

There are three basic kinds of recipe patterns that I cover in this ection.

- Rice (or other grain) with vegetables and/or beans

- Bean stews, soups or dals (Dal sounds trendier than pea soup)

- cold Rice (or other grain) and Vegetable salads

Master these three patterns and you master the core of main-course vegetarian cooking.

The Recipes

The recipes in this book are intended primarily as rough guides, examples of how the spices and other ingredients work well together. You can use them as-is, and you can use them as starting points for your own creativity. The recipes all reference which kind of spice pattern they use, to help you get comfortable with them.

Simple Daily Cooking

This is not primarily a book on creating elaborate feasts or gourmet meals to entertain and impress friends with, although you can certainly use these cooking techniques to do that if you wish. These are the kinds of meals I cook day in and day out, week after week. This is what my wife and I live on.

What I want to cover is simple and easy to prepare one-dish and two-dish meals that you can live on and enjoy. Simple enough to be do-able, varied enough to be tasty and enjoyable. That's why I cover just a few basic techniques that have a lot of room for variation without needing a lot of work.

Not About Replacing Meat

This book is not an attempt to produce imitation meat kinds of foods. Vegetable based burgers and meat substitutes are fun as a change of pace, but they are too expensive to serve as primary foods. I cover simple ways of cooking that let grains, vegetables and beans do what they do best, rather than trying to imitate something else.

(Optional) New Foods From Different Countries

In the recipes, I introduce a lot of food choices from different cuisines, primarily from India, Far East Asia, the Mediterranean, and Mexico. Unlike our regular American cooking, these cultures have highly developed vegetarian cuisines, and it only makes sense to use them.

A lot of these foods are becoming easily available in markets in larger cities, or are available online if you don't have easy access to stores that stock these foods. While use of foods from different cultures definitely increases the variety of your diet, they are not necessary to use the skills and recipes in this book.

Not a Comprehensive Cookbook

For space reasons, while this book does not cover all of the basic ways of cooking, I do provide enough information to prepare all the recipes and patterns I cover. I don't spend a lot of time on plain vegetable side dishes, since I usually prepare meals with the vegetables cooked in together with the grains or beans, and that is how I cover them here. I include a list of the cookbooks that I have found found helpful and interesting, the ones that I turn to regularly.

If you look through the list of recipes, you will see that I concentrate on grain and vegetable combination dishes, and on various bean dishes, since these form the core of the main-course food that makes up a satisfying vegetarian diet.

The Basics - Shopping, Meal Planning, Cooking

On Grains, Beans, Protein and Balance

The core of a satisfying vegetable-based diet is a balance of grains, beans and vegetables. This is true whether or not you include any eggs or dairy products. It also works well even if you still decide to eat some meat or fish. In my experience, I would roughly estimate the proportions of these foods in a satisfying diet as follows:

Grains - about 30% to 40%

Vegetables - about 40% to 60%

Beans - about 10% to 20%

Everything Else (fruit, dairy products, nuts, desserts) - maybe 10%

[Note 2021: I now eat a larger percentage of beans and nuts, and a bit smaller percentage of grains. I no longer regularly eat dairy other than butter, and I occasionally cook with fish or eggs. Trust your body's feedback, and eat whatever makes you feel best.]

A meat-based diet is anchored or built around the meat dish. That provides the center of the meal, and the rest of the meal is usually built to complement it.

In a vegetable-based diet, your grains and beans together form the hearty center of the diet. They are the dense and satisfying parts of the meal. If you try to eat too high a proportion of just vegetables without grains and beans, your meals will be unsatisfying and leave you feeling hungry and often ungrounded, spacey.

Your vegetables provide a lot of the variety of texture, color and taste. A diet without sufficient vegetables, with just grains and beans, is monotonous and unsatisfying in texture, and will leave you feeling stuffed and sluggish.

Get the proportions of these about right and you will have a diet that is nutritious, satisfying, that sits well and is easy to digest, and that leaves you feeling energetic and balanced. Also, these three together will give you a diet as simple, or as wildly varied, as you care to make it.

I have also found that grain, bean and vegetable-based meals leave me feeling centered, balanced and satisfied. Eat these foods enough and you will develop your own intuitive sense of meal balancing. This is useful, because if you have a sense of what it feels like to be centered and balanced, you will recognize it when you get off-balance. It's not much fun binging on sweet donuts and coffee once you recognize how off-balance you feel afterwards. Develop that feel for balance and your diet will become increasingly self-regulating. It just plain old feels better, and tastes better, to eat healthy and balanced meals.

About Protein

Francis Moore Lappe, in *Diet for a Small Planet*, popularized the concept of protein complementarity. Basically, with few exceptions, neither grains or beans by themselves are balanced and complete sources of protein. However, grains and beans complement and complete each other, so that these two foods eaten together provide complete and high quality protein.

The optimal proportion of grain to bean for best protein balance is around 3 to 1 or 4 to 1. Interestingly, I have found that this is about the proportion that these foods seem to digest the best.

A small amount of animal food - a little bit of cheese or yogurt, or egg - also complements grain protein.

Weekly Meal Planning and Background Cooking

Need for planning

Cooking economically, nutritiously and tastily takes some weekly thought and planning to pull off successfully. Being able to cook quickly and economically means thinking ahead to make sure you have good ingredients readily available to be able to put together a quick meal, and some already prepared dishes to use.

Not planning your dinner meal until an hour before does not encourage creativity and spontaneity. Instead it limits your choices to what you have on hand. If you don't take the time to think ahead you will find yourself being tempted to have pre-cooked convenience dinners sitting around, and they are not economical for money, for nutrition, or for taste. Or, more expensive yet, faced with a time pressure to cook and lack of good foods to cook with, you will be tempted to do take out, eat out, or home-delivery. That is not an efficient use of your food dollar.

Thinking and Planning Weekly

A week seems to be about the right unit of time to for making a general meal plan. I use the weekend to think out meals - with the general plan in place before I go shopping and not after! - then to do the shopping and major cooking.

Bean dishes, stews and soups lend themselves to being cooked in advance, and some stews like chili taste best on the second or third day. Grain salads for lunches, and some cabbage based vegetable salads, can also be prepared in large batches ahead of time.

Grains cook quickly enough that they can be cooked plain, in batches good for 2 or 3 days maximum, then kept on hand to combine with vegetables and other foods for quick dinners.

When you have main bean and grain dishes chosen as the framework for your week's meals, the one other thing you need is to have enough good quality vegetables around to quickly turn those grains and beans in to tasty and varied meals.

Shopping Weekly

In your main weekly shopping trip, your task is to get the foods and spices you need for the week's general meal plan.

Good quality fresh vegetables are the key ingredients to have around to make the meals work. You will probably have a combination of the main vegetables you always have around - things like onions, carrots, celery and such - combined with other veggies that vary by week or by season, according to what looks good at the market that day. You may end up building one or more meals around a vegetable that looked especially good that week.

Because good quality vegetables are so important to making meals work, I suggest that you make your main market for your weekly shopping run, the best source for good, fresh produce you can find.

Background Cooking

Preparing bean and vegetable based main-course stews and soups is a slow and time-consuming process, but it does not need to consume your time. With a little bit of forethought, it takes very little time and effort on your part, and the cooking can go on untended while you get on with the rest of your life. Many of the these foods can be prepared with methods of cooking that require little or no effort on your part.

Pre-soaking beans is a matter of washing them, putting them in water and letting them sit, all day or all night.

Cooking bean-based dishes like stews usually takes a little bit of work up front to assemble the ingredients, and then you can just let them alone to sit and cook. At the end of cooking time there is sometimes a little bit of work finishing up and adding final ingredients.

Slow cookers are wonderful for unattended background cooking, and bean based dishes get along well with slow cooking. Also, plain beans can be cooked completely unattended in a slow cooker. Beans freeze well, so it is a good idea to prepare a batch of beans and then freeze them in bags with the portion size you will want to cook with.

Summary - Here is the method I use to plan a week's meals.

• First, plan the main bean and vegetable stew dish, and/or maybe your grain based salad. Block out a very rough idea of meal plans for the week.

• Do the main shopping for the week, allowing for variation depending on what produce looks good.

• Get your big batch stew or grain salad prepared, and maybe prepare some plain beans to freeze, or as ingredients to mix in fresh dishes. Have enough grains cooked for 1-2 days ahead. Do as much background cooking as you can.

• Plan your meals for the week, taking into account the life-span of the vegetables you bought. Light green salads and dishes with perishable vegetables can be done earlier in the week, and the later meals can use more durable vegetables.

• Allow for a couple of easy to prepare change-of-pace dinners in the middle of the week using convenient on-hand ingredients.

• As the week wears on, perk up your leftover salads and stews with a bit stronger seasoning or extra garnishes.

General Guidelines for Effective Shopping

All of these guidelines are areas that I have learned by making mistakes. Hopefully they will save you time and money.

Shop low on the food processing chain. This means you are avoiding processed or precooked foods.

Buy whole and uncooked dry grains and beans. Regardless of where you shop these are the most economical foods you can buy. The same with vegetables - go for whole uncooked vegetables.

Even with convenience foods to keep around for quick meals, it is worth going for minimally processed.

Buy your food, even convenience food, plain and unspiced. I like to keep canned beans and frozen or canned vegetables around for quick meals, but I buy them plain, without prepared seasonings or sauces. They are most economical this way, and they give you a lot of flexibility in ways to use them. Pre-seasoned products like canned baked beans have much more limited flexibility of use.

Avoid most substitute animal or dairy products, things like soyburgers, tofu hot dogs or vegan ice cream. They may be fun as an occasional indulgence, but they are not an efficient use of your food dollar. The one exception I use regularly is good quality soy or rice or almond milk, which can be used in place of regular milk over cereals and in cooking.

Avoid buying empty foods. When you are trying to make every food dollar count, you really can't afford to spend a lot of money on food that is there just for taste or to fill up space without providing good nutritional value. This includes most pre-made soups and sauces.

Buy only good-quality ingredients. Shopping for food bargains is a good buy only if the food is nutritious and tasty to eat.

On the one hand, if a food is not nutritious, it is just taking up calories and space in your diet, and will probably leave you still wanting to eat more. On the other hand, if it doesn't taste good you probably won't get around to eating it.

Good quality oils are some of the more expensive food items that you will buy regularly. However, they can make a difference in the taste, and the amount of oil you use per dish is generally not that large so that a jar of oil goes a pretty long way.

Buy organic as much as you can afford. Organic food is more expensive than its conventionally grown counterpart, but it can sometimes be better quality. If you want to experiment for yourself, take a common food like onions, and cook with a conventional batch one week, and with an organic batch the next. See if you can tell the difference.

[Update 2021: I confess I am now disillusioned with the direction the organic food market has taken. It seems to have become an excuse for a high price markup. I am now much more likely to buy conventionally grown foods rather than their organic counterparts for that reason. Use your own judgment on this subject.]

Buy mainly vegetables that have a good storage life, and store them correctly. It's not much good buying high-quality organic vegetables if they sit and rot at the bottom of your refrigerator. If your are buying something like delicate greens, plan your meals so that you get around to eating them within a day or two.

Make plans to actually cook and use the foods you buy. I can't tell you how many cans and bags of miscellaneous food stuff I have accumulated over the years that has floated to the back of my pantry because I never got around to cooking with it, or how many wonderful fresh veggies have turned into mutants in my fridge because I never planned them into a meal.

Check out your local ethnic groceries for good quality foods at good prices. There are cuisines from all over the world that have highly developed traditional vegetarian foods and ways of preparing them, using all kinds of wonderful grains, beans and vegetables. It only makes sense to take advantage of them.

If you buy a food in a store where it is considered exotic or a trendy luxury, you will pay luxury prices. If you buy a food in a store where it is a regular part of the diet, you pay everyday prices.

When you can, buy foods at stores where that food is a basic part of that community's diet. For example, if you are going to make rice a big part of your diet, it makes sense to check out the groceries that cater to communities who already use a lot of rice as part of their regular diet. That includes Far East Asian (Japanese, Korean, Chinese, Vietnamese, Thai), Indian, Middle Eastern, Mexican. Each type of store will have the kinds of rice that community uses. You can sample small bags of different kinds and then go buy in bulk with the kind you really like.

When you do check out foods like this, be sure to compare prices and to check the quality by trying a small amount. Do not assume that food quality is either better or worse, or that prices are better or worse, because you are in an ethnic grocery. It varies widely.

Similarly, (and sadly), do not assume that food is higher quality because it is an expensive specialty item in a natural foods store or co-op. Vegetarian food is very trendy these days (especially organic!), and there are a lot of overpriced specialty and processed items on the shelves of natural foods stores and co-ops. Don't be hypnotized by the Natural Foods Mystique. Cheese isn't better just because it's unpronounceable and imported.

Buy in reasonable bulk - Once you know what kinds of rice, grains and beans you prefer, and about how often you use them, you can often get better prices if you buy in bulk. These are dried foods with very long shelf life, at least a year or two.

With spices, buy in reasonable bulk and avoid buying in little jars or cans - It is unfortunate, but supermarkets are about the worst places to buy spices for value and economy. You pay ridiculous prices for those little jars and cans. [Update 2021: unpackaged spices are getting harder to find - sigh. My experience is that spice prices are often much less expensive in Middle Eastern, Mexican, Asian or Indian groceries than they are in the main supermarkets.]

What to Buy Where

This is a list of some different kinds of markets, and some basic foods you can find there that are especially good food value and variety. These lists are not meant to be comprehensive, nor do they do justice to the wide variety of foods available in their cuisines. These are foods that I use all the time and that are not particularly exotic or weird tasting to most people.

Since quality of fresh produce varies wildly from market to market, the lists include mainly dried and canned foods and spices. I encourage you to check out any ethnic groceries in your town or city to see what their produce section is like, since you may find some very good selection and value.

Indian (Asian)

- basmati rice
- beans, peas, dals
- spices, chilis
- ghee (clarified butter)
- teas

Indian markets - Beans and peas are a regular part of their cuisine, and they have the most extensive and varied spice repertoire on the planet. Since they use spices so extensively their prices are usually very reasonable. They also have good quality basmati rice at very good prices since it is their main grain.

Middle Eastern

- basmati rice
- dried beans
- canned fava beans
- chilis
- bulghur (cracked wheat)
- pita bread
- spices
- teas
- olive & sesame oil
- dried dates and figs

Middle Eastern markets are good sources for basmati and other rices, for many spices, and for some dried beans and peas. You can also find bulghur or cracked wheat, and couscous which is another kind of wheat product. Canned fava beans are a good and economical convenience food. Some middle eastern markets also have good varieties of inexpensive black teas.

Oriental (Chinese etc.)

- rice - all kinds!

- some dried beans

- chilis and chili powders

- miso, soy sauce

- mock duck (wheat gluten)

- teas, esp. green, oolong

- sea vegetables (kombu, kelp, nori)

- good-tasting greens

Oriental markets are rice heaven. You can get short grain, medium grain, long grain, white rice and brown rice, and sticky rice. The short grain rice I find at oriental markets is my personal favorite for a versatile main grain. Mock duck or wheat gluten is available in small cans at good prices, and it tastes better than the pricey luxury kind you find in natural foods stores. Miso and soy sauce are salty fermented condiments widely used in Asian cooking. Those oriental markets that have good fresh produce sections often have selections of green leafy vegetables (bok choy, yu choy, nappa cabbage etc.) that cook up quickly and taste wonderful.

Mexican

- chilis, fresh and dried

- dried and canned beans

- spices (oregano, epazote)

- long grain white rice

Mexican markets - the little Mexican super-mercado near me has about a third of one wall devoted to different kinds of dried chilis, ranging in hotness from mild to incendiary. The other two-thirds of that wall is covered by inexpensive bags of all different kinds of spices. Along with long grain white rice, and dried and canned beans, some Mexican markets have good fresh produce sections, with fresh chilis and various common and uncommon vegetables.

One, Two and Three Dish Meals

The meals plans that I find satisfying follow simple patterns. These are the kind of meals that I can sit down to and eat a satisfying amount without the need to stuff myself, then get up and be able to go for some hours without feeling hungry or having the need to compulsively munch. They feel balanced to eat, and I feel balanced after I eat them.

Meals built around grains and vegetables, often complemented with beans, provide a satisfying eating experience. I like to have the grain be the largest part of the meal, with the proportion of grains to beans at least 3 to 1. These three foods together make up over 80% of my diet, with the other 20% devoted to Everything Else.

For meal planning purposes I divide them into one dish, two dish, and three dish meals.

One dish meals that I serve are almost invariably grain based, most often with rice, usually in combination with other ingredients including vegetables and beans or bean-based foods.

Some types of one dish meals include -

• rice and vegetables, sometimes including a complementary food like beans, tofu, or mock duck. This works for breakfast, lunch or dinner, and can be made endlessly varied by changing the spices or complementary vegetables, using more or less oil, cooking dry with just oil or wet with tomatoes or a sauce, and so on.

• cooked bulghur with vegetables - like the above.

• cooked pasta, either stirred up with sauteed vegetables, or with a thick sauce or stew that includes vegetables. Some tomato and pea soups with vegetables make a thick and satisfying pasta sauce that is as nutritionally rich as the pasta.

• cooked cereal, sometimes with apples, raisins and nuts, sometimes with soft vegetables like zucchini and onions. I know that our culture thinks of cereal as a sweet breakfast dish, but some cuisines like Indian also use it as part of dinner meals and include vegetables and spices.

- whole wheat toast, pita, or quickbread like cornbread. This is easiest of quick, light breakfasts with a little butter, peanut butter, or a dip appropriate for the bread.

With two dish meals , the grain dish often serves as a mild complement to the stronger tasting main dish. This is often a bean based soup or stew, often with a combination of vegetables, with rice or bread or some other grain served on the side. Having a good amount of vegetables in the bean stew makes the two dish meal more satisfying and balanced. When I have a bean dish with few vegetables I find myself wanting a salad or vegetable on the side to balance them out.

As a leftover or a lunch, I will often take a two-dish meal and turn it into a one-dish by pouring bean stew over rice to reheat in a microwave at work.

Sometimes the main dish is a hearty vegetable dish, like potatoes and cauliflower or a root vegetable dish, and it is complemented by bread or rice. Or, a light summer meal could be built around a fresh vegetable salad with bread or crackers on the side.

Three dish meals are most satisfying when I take a two-dish meal and add some kind of green vegetable on the side - a fresh green salad, or a lightly pickled cabbage salad, or cooked greens of some sort.

Lunch and Snack Ideas

How you plan on making lunches to take to work depends on whether or not you have access to a microwave oven for reheating dishes.

Access to a refrigerator is helpful, but not vital. Unlike animal based foods, most vegetable based dishes, like grain and vegetable salads or bean dips, can keep at room temperature for half a day without any problem. However, it's not a good idea to leave any food in a hot car.

If you have access to a microwave, taking a dish to reheat for lunch works quite well. One-dish lunches can be:

• grain and vegetable (and bean) sauteed dishes

• a thick soup or stew as a sauce over rice, pasta or another grain

• taking parts of a previous evening's dinner leftovers - In fact, it's a good idea, when you cook mid-week meals, to consider making extra and planning on using it for next day's lunch.

• a leftover cold rice and vegetable salad that you turn into a different dish by heating it.

If you like to have a simple side dish with your hot meal, some possibilities are:

• a dense salad like a cabbage-based salad, that travels and keeps well.

• raw vegetables like carrots and celery

• crackers

• raisins, fruit and nut trail mixes

Cold dishes can also make good lunches. For example:

• The most versatile one dish cold lunch is the rice and vegetable salad, or other grain based salad. You can keep this interesting on an ongoing basis by learning to vary the ingredients, the type of dressing, and the garnishes. A cold salad can also be 'perked up' on the 3rd or 4th day by adding some extra salt or lemon juice, or seeds or nuts, or grated cheese.

• Bean dip or sandwich spread works well. I find it preferable to bring the bean dip and bread or crackers in separate containers and combining them when you sit down to eat. The bread in pre-made bean and vegetable dishes can get soggy. If you want to do a bean dip and vegetable sandwich, have the vegetables in a separate bag and assemble it when you eat it. I think you will find that the bread tastes better that way.

• A vegetable salad can make a good light lunch with some substantial bread or roll on the side. A piece of cheese on the side can round out the meal if you wish.

Snack Foods - Assuming you don't want to waste money on empty snack foods out of vending machines at work, it helps to have some good, non-perishable munchie food around. Aside from pre-packaged snacks like granola bars, there are less expensive options for snacking.

• Trail mix and dried fruit and nuts are dense and substantial. You might want to be careful with eating too many nuts since they are very high in fat and calories.

• Instant oatmeal in packs is good if you have access to hot water to mix it with. This makes a good at-work breakfast also.

• Good dense crackers like rye krisp work well. It is worth avoiding crackers that are very salty or very sweet, since they can end up stimulating craving for other food rather than satisfying you.

• You can bring extra salad or raw vegetables with your lunch, or extra bean dip with crackers or bread to turn into an afternoon snack.

Basic Cookware

Here I want to mention the cooking implements that I find especially useful in preparing grains, beans and vegetables.

For most cookware I prefer stainless steel. I find non-stick cookware to be a nuisance since it calls for using only plastic utensils.

Rice cooking pot - Whatever else, a good rice pot needs to have a tight fitting lid to keep steam from escaping so the rice can cook evenly. A multi-ply bottom is useful to keep the rice from scorching, although you can work around that by using the next implement, which is -

Flame tamer - this is flat and disc-shaped, of metal with a handle. They are widely available in hardware and cookware stores. What a flame tamer does is to add a multi-ply layer between the pan and the heat source. The tamer is placed under the pot to distribute heat more evenly. It is a way to make inexpensive thin-bottomed cooking pans usable. The inexpensive $6 metal flame tamers work every bit as well as the luxury non-stick $40 ones. You will need to experiment with adjusting the heat level to the point that your food continues to cook at the desired level. I find it helpful to pre-heat a flame tamer before putting it under a pot, or getting the flame tamer ready on another burner and transferring the pot to that burner.

Pressure cooker - this is very useful for cooking brown rice, and all but indispensable for chickpeas and soybeans. Good pressure cookers are moderately expensive, but they will last a lifetime. The one part of a pressure cooker that can wear out is the rubber gasket, so I keep one or two spare gaskets on hand.

Steamer or double boiler - this is a pot with 2 or 3 levels, a lower level in which water can be boiled, and 1 or 2 upper levels with openings so that steam can get through, and a tight fitting cover. I like it for cooking basmati rice and white rice, and it is also convenient for cooking vegetables and reheating food. If you have a multi-level one you can cook more than one dish at once. Some Asian stores carry inexpensive steamer pots.

If you can't find a double boiler or are cooking in smaller amounts, a steamer basket that sits inside a covered pot works well.

Slow cooker - beans and vegetables cook well in a slow cooker, and they are useful for making one-pot meals that can be left to cook all day or overnight. They are not as useful for cooking grain, since grain needs to be more precisely timed. I have also found that grain and cereal sticks to the sides of the pot and does not cook as evenly as I would like.

Saute pan - most of the recipes I include involve sauteing vegetables and spices in oil. You need a wide bottomed pan with cover. If you can get it, it helps if the bottom is multi-ply or thick enough to distribute heat. Thin bottomed pans will burn easily. If you have only a thin-bottomed pan to work with, use a flame tamer under it to help distribute the heat.

Immersion Blender - This lets me puree soups and beans in the cooking pots. I find it much more convenient and easier to clean.

Steamer Basket - Very useful for quickly cooking vegetables.

Tips for Tasty Cooking

This is a chapter with notes on how to make food tasty, interesting and varied. Some of them are notes on general cooking, some on meal planning and variation, some on making leftovers interesting.

Use oil well to maximize flavor. It is the oil in foods that carries much of the taste, and that gives much of the satisfied feeling after eating.

If you skimp too much on your oil, you will probably find your cooking unsatisfying and not very tasty. It does no good to cut down on oil in cooking and then be craving fatty foods like milk and cheese to compensate. While you don't need to use large amounts of butter or lard, you can use a reasonable amount of healthy oils like olive or peanut, or ghee, or some butter for flavor, and come out with food that is very tasty, satisfying to eat, and healthy for you.

Part of the reason you need to allow for sufficient oil is that good soups, stews and sauces, depend on this cooking 'secret' - get your seasoning flavors, your spices and your condiment vegetables like garlic, ginger, onion, bell peppers and celery, cooked in the oil before adding the flavored oil to your cooking water or sauce.

That's the reason why the usual meat-based bean soup and bean recipes use a ham hock, bacon or sausage to cook with - they are all sauces of strongly flavored salty oil. That is also why most oil-free soups are so bland, and why spices that are just thrown into cooking water for soups are often flavorless.

Sauteing Onions - cook onions very slowly and they become smooth, sweet and rich tasting. Cook them on a higher flame and they are less sweet and have more of an edge, sometimes with a slightly scorched taste. The tastes have different uses. The rich, sweet taste is good for rich soups, stews and gravies. Onions cooked more quickly with more of an edge are good in tomato sauce, and with stronger tasting veggies and beans, especially with Mediterranean style spices.

Cooking grain with oil - adding the oil and spices to grain before it is cooked, gives a milder, subtler and more pervasive taste than if oil and spices are added after the grain is cooked, where the flavor coats rather than permeating the grains.

Varying tastes and textures - In meals with more than one dish you generally want the tastes and textures to complement rather than be too similar. For example, a rich wet stew is best complemented by a dry grain dish. Or, a very spicy rice dish could be complemented by a sweet and smooth tasting soup or stew, or vice versa.

If you think of tastes as being in 5 major categories - salty, sweet, sour, bitter, pungent - it's a good idea not to have the same taste dominant in all your dishes - so, a spicy sour stew with a sour cabbage salad and rice cooked with lemon juice would not work. Salty or sour dishes are complemented by mildly sweet dishes - and grains and most vegetables and beans are basically very mildly sweet.

Salty and sour in the same dish intensify each other - you will see them together often in the recipes. Using lemon juice or vinegar in your cooking lets you use less salt.

Salty and sweet tend to complement or balance rather than intensify each other. A little bit of sugar added to a dish with a primarily salty taste, like soy sauce, will mellow and smooth out the flavor a bit.

Hot dishes, those using peppers or chilis, are best complemented by bland grain dishes, and by smooth creamy side dishes like yogurt.

Varying Leftovers

This becomes very important when you are cooking ahead a lot, and making stews or rice dishes to last for 3 to 5 days. Here are some suggestions.

• Vary the side dish. If you have a bean and veggie stew, have it with plain rice one day, with toast another day, over rice another day.

• By the 3rd day, vary or 'perk up' your leftover by adding a little extra seasoning - a little extra salt and lemon to make the taste a little sharper often helps. An extra touch of cayenne or pepper can also liven it up. Or, add a garnish like seeds, nuts or grated cheese.

• For a rice and veggie dish you can make a half-new dish by sauteing some veggies with spices and adding the leftovers to that. A cold rice salad can be turned into a hot rice and vegetable dish with a little extra oil, cooked onion and spices.

• If you cook ahead with whole beans, say for a stew, make enough beans that you can keep some of them plain, to be mixed in veggie and rice quick sauteed dishes.

• Keep an interesting bean dip around to have as a snack with bread, or as a complementing side dish with a plain grain dish.

• When you make rice for a meal, cook your rice plain and make extra, so that you have it available as an ingredient to stir into a fresh dish.

• If you are planning a week's worth of meals, make Tuesday or Wednesday your 'Eat Something Else' day as a change of pace, and do a quick cooking meal with a convenient food like mock duck, or pre-cooked beans with rice and veggies with a different spice pattern. Pasta also makes a good change of pace. You might also consider having a soft cooked cereal like cream of wheat or rice, either sweet like a breakfast cereal or cooked with soft vegetables and spices.

• Use a topping, dip or relish as a side accent to vary the taste of dishes.

Expand your thinking about appropriate foods, especially for breakfast or dinner. For instance, I often like to start the day with a vegetable soup for breakfast, and cooked cereal makes a wonderful and warming quick dinner.

Adapting recipes that use meat

A lot of cookbooks use meat as a main flavoring for soups, stews and sauces. I am thinking especially of bean dishes here, since it is very

41

difficult to find bean or pea recipes in most cookbooks that don't rely on ham, bacon, salt pork or sausage for the primary broth seasoning. With a lot of recipes like that, just leaving out the meat leaves out most of the flavor, and that doesn't make a satisfying dish.

If you think in terms of types of tastes, the meat in soups and stews basically adds a strong salty taste, sometimes spiciness, and almost always a good amount of fat or oil. In other words, these soups rely on seasoning in oil for their primary taste. Foods like bacon and ham, which are cured, often add a sour taste also. Some meats also add a smoked flavor.

So, to replace the meat in such recipes, you need seasoned and flavorful oil, some kind of salty condiment, and sometimes a sour taste. This underlines the importance, when making meat free soups and stews, of getting your primary flavoring into the oil by sauteing your vegetables and spices before adding them to the stew. That should be sufficient to guarantee a flavorful dish.

Most of the recipes in this book use sauteed vegetables and spices, salt or a salty condiment like soy sauce, and often a sour condiment like lemon juice or vinegar. This combination effectively replaces the need for meat-based flavoring.

So, when you want to try a soup or stew recipe you see that uses meat for flavoring, think about ways to add flavorful oil. You can do this by taking some of the vegetables the dish calls for and sauteing them before adding to the soup, or by adding spices to the oil. Garlic, ginger and fennel in oil can add a spicy sharpness that replaces the spiciness from the seasoned meat, and the three together smell like good sausage spices while you are cooking.

If you really enjoy the smoked flavor from meats, using whole dried chipotle chili is a way of adding good quality smoked flavor. Leave the chili whole and remove it before serving and you will get a good smoky taste with very little hotness.

Recipes that call for chicken or other broth - ignore it and use water. Broth is a way of getting a flavorful liquid. Once you know about getting spices and flavors into your cooking oil, look for ways to adjust where spices are added. Also, remember that vegetables like onions and celery that are just thrown into the cooking water add less appealing flavor than if they are first sauteed until soft, even in just a small amount of oil.

Cooking for the Seasons

The longer I eat a grain and vegetable based diet, the more sensitive I become to how the food I eat affects how I feel and function, and how it ties in with the season of the year and the weather. Tuning your cooking to the season and weather is a matter of paying attention to how you feel after you eat, and being sensitive to the kinds of foods your body seems to like in different seasons.

If you have difficulty relating to this idea, try to picture yourself coming home on a 100 degree humid autumn day to a steaming bowl of oven-baked steel cut oats. Just the thought of it makes me sweat.

When I go shopping in January, seeing a shopping cart ahead of me filled with lettuce and light greens, fruit flavored yogurt and oranges is enough to start me shivering.

Here I want to talk briefly about using foods appropriate for the weather and season. That is partly a matter of grains that fit the seasons, and partly a function of what vegetables are available.

I live in Minnesota, so I will start with the season that takes up five months of our calendar year, which is -

Winter - This is the time of the year for dense, hearty, seriously warming foods. Buckwheat and steel cut oats are good winter grains, and oven-baked steel cut oats is the meal of choice for dinner on days with below-zero windchill. I use short grain brown rice more in cold weather than in warm since it is heavy, soft, dense and comforting. It is a good time to go heavy on thick soups and stews with a lot of dense

43

root vegetables like turnips, parsnips, rutabaga, and the dense winter squash that keep until winter. Raw foods are minimized or eliminated, and I find myself wanting more salt and stronger seasoning.

Spring - Time to lighten up a bit. Good bitter spring greens like mustard greens, dandelion greens, asparagus and fiddlehead fern (if you can find it, it's like asparagus only better) taste good this time of year either raw or lightly cooked. Bulghur is a good grain year round, but seems to work the best in Spring. It's a nice time to lighten up on salt and heavy seasonings and maybe use a bit more lemon and sour tastes to compensate.

Sauteed grain dishes and stews can use less heavy root vegetables and more lighter veggies like zucchini.

Summer - Here the need is for light and cooling foods, and probably just plain eating lighter. Dense stews are out, and cold rice and grain salads are in. Light and cooling green salads work better this time of year than any other. Oven baking vegetables is out and lightly steaming is in. It's a good time to go light on salt and strong seasoning also, although hot chilis are the exception

• most cuisines that make heavy use of hot chilis come from warm climates. Light and easy to digest grain foods like couscous and pasta work well also, and corn fits the season. Basmati rice, which is quite light and fluffy, works well. I also find myself eating more fruit in summer than any other time of year, since most fruit is cooling to eat - that shopping cart I mentioned full of lettuce, yogurt and oranges is a summer cart.

Autumn - Here the cooking is ruled by the glorious autumn harvest, especially the wonderful varieties of squash available, some of which won't make it to the winter. Time to switch away from the light salads and cold lunches and start having more stews and denser cooked meals.

Also, time to enjoy as much of a variety of seasonal vegetable dishes as possible before they disappear for the long winter.

Through this whole cycle of the seasons there are the core foods, like rice and the main vegetables like onions, carrots and such, that work well year round. They may be prepared a bit more lightly in summer and a bit more heavily seasoned in winter, but they serve as a kind of core stabilizing base to the diet throughout the year.

Other Cookbooks

Disclaimer: There are a lot of vegetarian cookbooks out there, and a lot of them I just don't like. Most vegetarian cookbooks in America rely extremely heavily on dairy products, to the point that well over 75% of the recipes call for dairy in some form. Many others spend too much time on recipes that try to act like or replace meat-based cuisine. Others are oil and salt phobic to the point of being taste phobic. And, far too many vegetarian cookbooks are too complex, use too many expensive ingredients, or seem to be aimed at affluent people with a lot of time and money on their hands who like to impress their friends.

Thes are my personal favorite cookbooks, the ones I have learned the most from and that I keep coming back to.

Jaffrey, Madhur, **Madhur Jaffrey's World Vegetarian.** New York, Clarkson Potter, 1999. My favorite cookbook. Very detailed and comprehensive, gives vegetarian cuisine from around the world.

Madison, Deborah, **Vegetarian Cooking for Everyone.** New York, Broadway Books, 1997. A kind of vegetarian Joy of Cooking, basic and comprehensive. Unlike many American vegetarian cookbooks that overdose on milk and cheese, she uses some dairy without relying heavily on it.

Basic Ingredients and Cooking Instructions

Grains

If you want to have a way of eating that is mainly made up of quality vegetable foods, you will need to have good quality grains as a central part of your diet. Grains have a calming, centering, and settling or grounding effect, and leave a satisfied feeling after eating, in a way that no other single food does.

Here is a list of basic grains, and grain-based foods, that I like to keep around at all times. I divide them up into Rice and Other.

Let's take a quick look at the main grains, one at a time.

Rice

Rice comes in short, medium or long grain, and each type cooks up to a different texture. White rice has the exterior hull removed, and brown rice has the hull intact.

Long grain white rice, which is the most commonly used kind of rice in American cooking, usually cooks up relatively lightly. When you have a diet where the meat dish serves as the center of the meal, you want your grain to be light to balance the meat.

When you move to a vegetable-based diet, you don't have that heaviness of the meat to deal with, so the grain literally needs to carry more weight in the meal. Short grain rice is denser and heavier than long grain rice. It feels more substantial to eat, so it can help to lend weight to a vegetable based meal.

Short grain white rice also has a distinctly different texture than long grain rice, heavier and stickier, and you may find it takes some getting used to. The denser texture can be very satisfying, especially when it is cooked with vegetables or eaten with a sauce. I find that short grain white rice is easier to digest, quicker to cook, and more versatile than brown rice.

Brown rice is denser and heavier than white rice, and it can also be a lot chewier.

Some people (including me) find white rice easier to digest than brown rice. if you find brown rice hard to digest, soaking the brown rice in cold water for an hour or more before cooking aids in digesting the rice. This makes the rice cook to a very soft texture, not at all like the light fluffiness of long grain white rice. It works well cooked in with sauteed vegetables as a dense main course.

Basmati rice is a staple of Indian and some Middle Easter cooking. It is lighter in texture than regular white rice. When I want a light and fluffy main grain to balance a substantial bean dish, vegetable dish, or a bean or pea soup, good quality basmati rice has an aromatic quality and delicate taste that are wonderful.

The rice you cook can also vary by season and weather. You might consider using light textured basmati rice more in the summer and in warmer weather, and heavy, dense and warming short grain brown rice more in the winter.

The kind of rice that you choose as your main rice may partly depend on the kind of markets near you. Oriental groceries (Chinese, Japanese, Korean and others) have the widest variety of types of rice including short, medium and long grain, white and brown. Indian groceries carry basmati rice, Middle Eastern stock basmati, parboiled and long grain rice. Mexican and markets stock long grain white rice.

Other Grains

Bread and bread products It is worth having good whole grain bread around, to serve as a side dish of toast to complement a vegetable or bean and vegetable dish for a quick meal. I keep a loaf in the fridge at all times that toasts well. I also like to keep flatbreads like flour tortillas around and use them for quick light sandwiches.

Bulghur, or cracked wheat, is a partially cooked whole wheat product. It cooks up in about 15 minutes, so it is good for quick dinners. Bulghur is the grain in tabouli, the Middle Eastern parsley and vegetable salad.

Couscous is another quick-cooking wheat product, that cooks up to make a lighter and less substantial dish, good in warm weather. Couscous is also good cooked in fruit juice as a dessert or as a light breakfast cereal.

Oatmeal, Steel Cut Oats For good cooked oats, one brand stands out - McCann's Irish Steel Cut Oats. [2021 Update: I would add Bob's Red Mill for grain products in general, including oats.] If you enjoy oats, get it. It can be cooked stovetop, or in a slow cooker, or baked in the oven. It goes well with fruits, nuts and spices like cinnamon and nutmeg, or it can be cooked with vegetables like zucchini and carrots and serve as a main grain dish with a dark onion gravy. Cooked oats are rich and very warming, and make a good winter meal.

Oatmeal also makes a good cereal, and cooks up quickly. Oatmeal can also be used to add a creamy richness to soups.

Cream of wheat, cream of rice, cereals - they're not just for breakfast anymore. These are quick cooking, 2 to 10 minutes depending on the coarseness of the grind. Aside from being breakfast cereals, they can also be cooked with vegetables and Indian spices to make a fast main course grain dish.

Buckwheat, a whole grain, cooks up in just 15 minutes. It is at its best roasted, and it is worth buying buckwheat roasted to save time. It is a very warming, winter grain with a dusky flavor that goes well with onion gravy.

Quinoa, pronounced 'KEEN-wa' is becoming increasingly popular. It is native to South America, and is one of the few grains that is a good complete protein source by itself. Quinoa has a very bitter protective coating, so it needs to be well washed and rinsed before cooking. It cooks up in about 15 minutes to a very soft, cereal-like texture, with distinctive little rings around each grain.

Barley is rarely eaten by itself, but is often used as a grain in soups, or cooked in combination with rice.

Pasta is a widely known grain dish that makes a nice change of pace. I list this as an alternate grain.

Grain cooking Directions

Basically grain is cooked by heating it with just enough water or other liquid so that all of the liquid is absorbed when the grain is done. (Pasta is an exception, and is typically boiled and then drained.)

With any of these forms of cooking grain, with the exception of ground cereal, it is important to not uncover, stir or disturb the grain once it is covered, until the full cooking time is elapsed.

There are a few basic ways of cooking grains.

Steeping: The all -purpose method. Bring the water to a boil on the stovetop, add the grain, stir and bring back to a boil, cover tightly and reduce the flame to very low until all liquid is absorbed. If the bottom of your pot is thin and the grain tends to scorch, you can use a flame tamer under the pot - experiment with getting the flame just high enough that the water keeps simmering, but low enough that it doesn't burn.

With rice, if you add the rice to cold water and then boil and steep, the rice will come out heavier and denser than if you boil the water first and then add the rice.

If you use an electric stove, take into account that the temperature of the healing coils does not rapidly shift, so the rice can end up scorching on the bottom of the pot. The best way I have found to deal with that is to use TWO burner rings, one set for the boil, the other for the simmer. When the rice water is boiling and hot enough, move it over the second, lower burner.

Steaming: Put the grain and warm water in a covered dish and put the dish in the upper half of a double boiler or steamer pot. This cooks a bit more slowly than steeping, but it is pretty much impossible to burn the grain, so cooking a bit longer doesn't hurt. When you get it to work this is a great way to cook basmati rice. [Note 2021: I find the cover on the steamer needs to close very tightly for this to work. If you do it wrong you can end up with underdone crunchy rice.]

Pressure Cooking: Probably the best and quickest way to cook short grain brown rice. Add the rice, water and salt to the pressure cooker, bring up to pressure, then cook until all liquid is absorbed and grain is done. Use a flame tamer if necessary, as in steeping, and adjust the flame to just enough to keep pressure up. Allow pressure to drop.

Baking: A slow method that produces a very dense and warming grain. I use it for steel cut oats and sometimes for short grain brown rice. Add the grain and water to a covered ovenproof dish and bake at 425 degrees until all liquid is absorbed and grain is done. If the grain is cooked before the liquid is gone, stir and return to the oven uncovered and bake another 5 minutes or until the dryness you want. Baking grain takes up to 50% longer than steeping.

Here are my favorite ways to cook the various grains.

Short grain white rice - my all-purpose everyday rice. 1½ c water to cup of rice, plus ½ tsp salt. Boil the water, add the rice, then cover and steep the rice for 15 minutes and let sit for 10 minutes, or steep for 20 and let sit for 5. It can also be steamed for 35-40 minutes.

Long grain white rice - Proportion 2 to 1 water to rice, with ½ to 1 tsp salt, add to boiling water and steep for 25 minutes, let sit for 5 minutes.

In a pressure cooker I find that white rice needs a short time under pressure but then time to sit. I boil the water, same proportions as above, bring up to pressure then cook for only 3 minutes. Turn off the heat and let the pressure come down by itself, which takes maybe 15-

20 minutes. Total cooking time is the same but much less time is spent with the heat source on.

Brown rice - Proportion 2 to 1 water to rice, with ½ to 1 tsp salt, pressure cook at high for 20 minutes, then turn off heat and allow to come down at its own pace - I let it sit about another 20 minutes. With steeping it seems to take closer to an hour, with steaming closer to 90 minutes. This makes the rice very soft and dense, and mildly sweet tasting. Cooking brown rice with less water or for less time makes it too chewy for my taste.

If you have trouble with indigestion or gas when you eat brown rice, try soaking the rice in cold water for at least an hour, then letting it drain for at least 15 minutes before cooking. This makes the rice cook up softer and heavier, and easier to digest.

Basmati rice - Steaming works well, and stovetop steeping as described above for long grain white rice works also. Steamed basmati comes out very light, fluffy and aromatic. Basmati rice is often soaked before cooking. Here's the procedure for steaming. Note that, for this to work, the top on the steamer must be very snug.

Proportion 1½ to 1 water to rice, with ½ to 1 tsp salt. Soak the basmati in warm water for at least 10 minutes, drain and reserve the liquid, and let sit in a strainer for at least 15 minutes. Combine the rice with the warmed soaking water, salt, and a pat of butter if desired, and steam for 35 minutes. The cooked rice can sit in the steamer over a very low flame for awhile after it is done without harm.

For stovetop steeping, proceed as for steaming and cook about 20 minutes and let sit for 5 minutes. The rice will not be as light and fluffy as steamed basmati.

Quinoa - Wash and rinse well in cold water - I let it sit in cold water around 5 minutes. Strain in a very fine mesh strainer - the grains of quinoa are quite small. Steep as usual, proportion 2 to 1 water to grain, with ½ to 1 tsp salt, for 15 minutes.

Bulghur - Proportion 1½ to 1 water to grain, with ½ to 1 tsp salt, or up to 2 to 1 for a softer grain. Steep for 15 minutes.

Buckwheat - Proportion 2 to 1 water to grain, with ½ to 1 tsp salt, steep 15 minutes.

Steel-Cut Oats - Proportion 4 to 1 water to grain, with ½ to 1 tsp salt.. Steep for 30-45 minutes, or bake covered at 425 degrees for 45 minutes to an hour. If the oats are soaked in water overnight, the cooking time steeped is reduced to 15 or 20 minutes.

Beans

Where grains can serve as the center of a meat-free diet, beans are your main protein complement. Grains and beans, eaten together, provide balanced and assimilable protein. There are such a wide variety of beans that varying your bean cooking, while keeping the grain part of your cooking simpler, can help keep your meals interesting.

This is a list of the main beans I like to keep around.

Red lentils are the fastest cooking of all beans. They are smaller than regular lentils and are pinkish red when raw, and cook up a medium brown color. They require no soaking, cook up in less than 30 minutes, and are easy to digest. Red lentil vegetable soups make good quick meals. I also use red lentils along with other beans in stews since they dissolve quickly and serve to thicken the sauce.

Split peas, either yellow or green, make a good base for thick and hearty soups with vegetables and sometimes grains like barley or rice, and they are very widely available. They do not need soaking and cook up quickly, in about 45 minutes. They go well with strong tastes and thick textured root vegetables.

Moong dal is not commonly found at your regular supermarket. I find them at Indian, or Far East Asian, or Middle Eastern groceries. They are split and hulled mung beans, are about the size of red lentils, and are a bright orange yellow in color, raw and cooked. Like red lentils they need no soaking and cook up quickly, and they are a wonderful base for simple but rich soups with just a vegetable or two. This is one of the few 'exotic' ingredients that I recommend you consider making a regular part of your food on hand. If you buy them by mail or internet , make sure you get split and hulled moong dal, and not the whole mung beans. You can tell by the color, since the skin of mung beans is a dark green.

Lentils are another good, easy to digest and versatile beans. You will find brown, green or black lentils, but they can be used interchangeably. Lentils can be soaked but do not need it, and they cook on the stovetop in about 45 minutes. They are also easy to digest, and are sturdier and more hearty than their red lentil cousins. They can be used in soups or stews, or pureed and made into a satisfying dip, or drained from their cooking water and mixed into salads or other vegetable or rice dishes.

Black eyed peas are soaked sometimes but do not need it. They cook up in less than an hour. With a pressure cooker, black eyed peas are done in 12 minutes without soaking. They are not a strong tasting bean, and they go well in simple dishes, with just a few herbs and maybe some onions and a touch of butter.

Chickpeas or garbanzo beans are one of the best tasting and most versatile beans, and are used all over the world. They are one of the longest cooking beans, requiring soaking, and taking 20 minutes in a pressure cooker, or 3 to 4 hours stovetop to become tender. Once cooked, they have a wonderful sweet and nutty taste. They go well in soups, with rice and other vegetables, or drained in salads, and they are the base of hummus which is a popular Middle Eastern bean dip made with chickpeas. The cooking liquid from chickpeas is golden and sweet and makes a wonderful base for soups, with or without the whole beans.

Pinto beans and kidney beans require soaking, and cook up in less time than chickpeas - pressure cooker time is around 12 minutes. They are a large, hearty, rich-tasting bean, and are good in hearty stews with tomato and vegetables, in chili, or drained and used with rice or vegetables.

Black beans are at their best in black bean soup cooked Mexican style with the dried herb epazote, and with dried chipotle chili to lend the soup a smoky flavor. Good thick black bean soup is tasty and very addicting. Black beans also work well in chili or in soups with tomato. They require soaking and cook in about the same time as pintos.

Fava beans are a staple of Middle Eastern cooking. Favas have a very tough outer skin and need to be peeled after cooking, so I rarely buy them dried whole. Split and peeled dried fava beans make a thick and tasty alternative to split pea soup. Canned favas are inexpensive, ready to use and very tasty. They work very well in Mediterranean seasoned bean and vegetable or bean and rice dishes.

Aduki beans are a bean commonly used in Oriental cooking, where they are often mashed and combined with sugar to make a sweet paste that tastes surprisingly similar to chocolate, and used as a filling in desserts. I have used it with chopped pistachios, wrapped in a soft bread like lefse, with a real or tofu whipped cream topping. It also makes what my daughter calls a curiously addicting ginger and bean dip, and I include a recipe for that dip.

Making Beans Easy To Digest

Like many people, over the years I have found that I sometimes have problems digesting beans, both with gassy stomach pains (which bother me) and with flatulence, which is a highbrow term for farting (which bothers the people downwind from me). There are a combination of things that, taken together, make beans easy to digest.

- pre-soaking
- very thorough cooking

- boiling beans hard for 5 minutes before main cooking method

- not adding salt or acidic foods until beans are thoroughly soft

- supporting spices

- combinations and proportions of beans with grains

- chewing and savoring

- acclimating - eat smaller amounts until you are more used to them.

First, and very important with any bean, pick over the dried beans, discarding any small stones or foreign matter. I pour them out ¼ cup at a time on a dinner plate and spread them out flat with my fingers. Once they are picked clean, rinse very thoroughly.

Pre-Soaking - For all but a few, very easy to digest beans (moong dal from India, lentils, and black-eyed peas) I find that pre-soaking the beans seems to make a difference in digestibility. Here's how you do it.

- Pick over and clean the beans.

- Next, cover with water, at least a 3 to 1 water to beans, since they swell up.

- Now just let the beans sit at room temperature, at least 8 hours or overnight.

- Note that I do not discard the soaking water. As far as I can tell it does not affect digestibility, and keeping the soaking water improves the taste and color.

Quick soak method - after cleaning, put beans in water and bring to a boil, and boil them for about 5 minutes, then let them sit for 1 hour or more. Whichever method of soaking you use, drain and discard the soaking water and rinse the beans thoroughly before adding fresh water and cooking.

Very Thorough Cooking - This is the single most important factor in making beans easily digestible. Beans should be cooked until they are soft all the way through, with no firmness or crunchiness. Firm and crunchy beans look good on a plate but are hard to digest.

Boiling Hard Before Main Cooking Method - Whether you pressure cook or slow cook beans, it is a good idea to bring them to a rolling boil without pressure for about 5 minutes before using your main cooking method. This seems to help with digestion and can dramatically shorten the cooking time, especially when using a slow cooker. The purpose of the hard boiling seems to make sure that the beans and water are thoroughly hot before lowering heat to the main cooking method.

Wait on Salt and Acidic Ingredients - Both salt and acidic ingredients such as tomatoes interfere with the process of beans becoming tender, so hold off adding them to the beans until they are thoroughly cooked. [Note 2021: I am now not sure if you need to wait on adding salt, but it is definitely true that adding anything acidic must be avoided until the beans are completely tender.]

Digestive Spices - Indian cooking uses ginger, turmeric, and sometimes fennel and asafetida to cook with beans to make them more digestible. I especially recommend ginger and turmeric. If you use a small amount with the beans while you cook them, they aid with digestion but do not dominate the flavor.

Japanese and far East Asian cooking uses a piece of kombu or kelp, which is a kind of seaweed, cooked in with beans. It seems to help make beans a bit softer, thickens their cooking liquid a bit, and also enhances their flavor. I usually throw a small piece of kombu in with the cooking water, and then add ginger, turmeric and sometimes fennel.

Those are the main spices that I can confirm assist with digesting beans. I use them constantly, and I can tell the difference in digestibility when I leave them out.

Combinations and Proportions of Foods - I have found that what foods I combine the beans with, and the proportion of beans to other food, affects how easily they digest.

Beans go really well with different forms of grains - rice, pasta, and breads. They seem to work best together when the amount of grains equals or exceeds the amount of beans. Grains and beans are usually found together in traditional cuisines around the world.

When I make rice and bean combined dishes, I like the proportion of rice to beans to be 3 to 1 or more. When I make bean and rice salads that are 1 to 1 proportion, I find myself wanting a piece of bread on the side to balance. It's almost instinct by now to want to balance the beans with grain.

Interestingly, this 3 to one proportion of grains to beans matches the proportion for best combined complete protein.

Chewing and Savoring - VERY IMPORTANT! - Both beans and grains are foods where a lot of the digestive process takes place in the mouth. Unlike meat, they are not foods that lend themselves to being gulped unchewed. Chewing beans and grains thoroughly, or savoring dal or pea soup broth in the mouth before swallowing, greatly reduces gas and makes digesting them a lot smoother. It also brings out more of their flavor and makes eating them more enjoyable.

Cooking With Canned Beans - When you use beans from a can or jar, make very sure that the beans are thoroughly cooked, soft and not crunchy. Drain and rinse the beans before adding them to whatever dish you are making. This makes them easier to digest. It gives the dish you add them to a cleaner and fresher taste, and it also seems to lengthen the time the leftovers stay good tasting in the fridge. You can also use spices like ginger and turmeric to aid digestion. [2021 update - I now no longer drain canned beans when I use them in a wet dish, but I do drain them when using them in salads.]

Summary - If I had to pick out the absolutely essential things to keep in mind, they are -

• thorough cooking

• eating with grains

• chewing and savoring

Bean Cooking

Basically, beans are cooked by combining them with water and cooking until done. Do not add salt or acidic ingredients until the beans are completely tender.

Beans can be simmered stovetop, or slow cooked, or pressure cooked. The cooking times are for simmering unless noted. I talk about slow cookers and beans later in this section.

Cooking times for beans can vary according to how old the beans are, how hard your water is, and how high a heat to cook them over, so you will need to play around to find optimal cooking times for your equipment and style.

With whole beans like pintos or kidneys, using too much excess water in the cooking seems to make the beans split more. This is okay if you are doing a stew, but may not be what you want if you intend to drain the beans and use them sauteed with rice or veggies.

For all the beans except red lentils and moong dal I suggest boiling the beans for 5 minutes before reducing the heat to a low rolling boil and finishing the cooking time. I sometimes add a 4 inch stick of kelp, ½ tsp turmeric, and sometimes ½ tsp chopped ginger and/or 1 tsp fennel seeds cooked in with the beans to aid with digestion without strongly affecting the taste.

Slow-Cooking Beans

Slow cooking beans is very close to the way beans were traditionally cooked, very slowly in a pot on the back of the stove or fire. It is almost impossible to overcook beans in a slow cooker, and I have found they are more likely to come out tender but still intact.

When I cook a batch of beans on the weekend, I like to let the beans soak Saturday during the day, then let them cook overnight Saturday. Sunday morning my beans are cooked and ready to use as is or to combine in other dishes.

There are a few things I find useful to keep in mind when using a slow cooker with beans.

• Bring the beans to a boil in their cooking water before adding to the slow cooker with the other ingredients. This makes for a much shorter cooking time than adding beans and water cold to the slow cooker, up to 2-3 hours shorter. It also guarantees that the beans and water are hot enough for them to thoroughly cook.

• Bring any additional liquid to a boil first before adding to the beans during cooking.

• Use a tablespoon or two of oil in with the beans, especially if you add spices. This seems to enhance the richness and distribution of flavor.

• As with any other method of cooking beans, add salt or acidic ingredients only after the beans are tender. Allowing 10 minutes more cooking time after adding the salt is enough. When adding diced tomatoes, you may want to allow up to another hour, although that can be shortened by pre-heating the tomatoes before adding them to the cooker.

• Go lighter on the spices with a slow cooker than with stovetop cooking.

• If you are using sauteed vegetables in with the beans, they can be added at the start of cooking if you hold off on adding salt. Sauteed veggies can also be added for about the last hour of cooking.

I group the beans here according to similar cooking times, from quickest to longest cooking.

Red lentils, moong dal - no soaking needed, about 3 or 4 to 1 or more proportion water to beans. These cook completely in ½ hour to 45 minutes at the most. I almost never slow-cook these beans

Red lentil/moong dal shortcut - put the beans, water (and turmeric and kombu if desired) in a pot in the morning, bring to a boil, cover and remove from the heat. By dinner hour, heat up the dish and the red lentils/dal should be cooked through within 10 minutes.

Lentils (brown, green, black), Blackeyed Peas - soaking optional. Proportion 4 to 1 water to peas, cook for 50 minutes to an hour. For slow-cooking, Blackeyed peas or lentils, presoaked, cook in 6-7 hours. Without soaking, they slow-cook overnight, around 10-12 hours. Blackeyed peas get quite soft when slow-cooked, but in my experience lentils slow-cook firm and done but not soft.

Split Peas - Soaking is not necessary. Proportion at least 4 to 1 water to peas, probably more since they are usually used as a stew base. Cook for 45 minutes to an hour more or less, depending on whether you want them tender to falling apart. I have found that split peas just do not get soft enough when slow-cooked - they definitely cook to doneness, but not to falling-apart softness that makes a good thick soup. If you want to slow-cook these peas, try boiling them for 10 minutes first and then adding them to the slow cooker overnite.

Pintos, Kidneys, Black Beans, Navy Beans, Mayocoba beans - Always pre-soak. Proportion 4 to 1 water to beans, simmer for 2 hours, or pressure cook about 50 minutes. For slow-cooking, presoaked and pre-boiled for 10 minutes, these beans cook in around 7-10 hours.

Chickpeas, Soybeans - the longest cooking beans. Always pre-soak. Proportion 4 to 1 water to beans, simmer for 3-4 hours, or pressure cook about 20 minutes. Slow-cooking works really well with chickpeas and soybeans; presoaked and pre-boiled for 5 minutes, these beans cook in around 10-12 hours, or not much more than kidney beans.

Pressure - Cooking Beans

This is now my favorite way of cooking many beans. It cuts cooking time by a lot.

Using a pressure cooker with beans, it is VERY important that the pot be less than half full. Fill it more than that and there is a risk that a bean skin could clog the pressure vent, and cause the emergency pressure valve to blow off.

It is also a good idea to add a little bit of oil to the cooking water. That seems to reduce the foaming that can cause problems.

Split peas and other dals that are cooked until they are completely soft are better cooked on the stove top. The pressure cooker works best for beans that you want to keep their shape. It is a good idea to let the pressure on the pot drop gradually, rather than speeding it up by putting it under running water. That last bit of time the beans sit in the pot seems to be necessary.

Proportion of water to beans is about 3 to 4 cups water to 1 cup dried beans. If you are new to pressure cooking beans I would start with the higher amount, and then reduce if you find the beans have a lot of cooking liquid left when they are done. The beans can be refrigerated in the cooking liquid until you use them.

As usual, do not add salt or any acidic condiments like vinegar until AFTER the beans are cooked. Avoiding acidic is especially important.

The cooking times are fairly simple.

Black-Eyed Peas - unsoaked, these cook up in 12 minutes after full pressure is reached. This is my go-to quick bean meal if I haven't prepared.

Most Beans - this includes pinto, kidney, mayocoba, black beans, aduki beans, white beans like great northern or canellini. These beans, pre-soaked, cook up in about 12 minutes after full pressure is reached.

Garbanzo Beans/Chickpeas, or Soybeans. Pre-soaked, cooking time is about 20 minutes at full pressure.

Vegetables

I Always Have Around

- onions
- carrots
- cabbage (green and red)
- celery
- diced tomatoes (canned), tomato sauce
- garlic

I Use Often

- potatoes
- bell peppers
- collard greens, kale
- zucchini
- radishes (white or red)
- frozen corn and peas

I Use Occasionally

- parsnips, turnips, beets
- winter squash (seasonal)
- lots of others, depending on season and availability

Tomatoes I prefer to keep around as cans of diced tomatoes or tomato paste, rather than buying fresh. This is because I almost always find fresh whole tomatoes, even organic, to be disappointing and relatively tasteless. Cherry tomatoes are an exception, and are very good in salads. I use diced tomatoes a lot as part of a soup base with beans, or mixed in with rice and vegetables.

New and Interesting Vegetables

Some of the recipes include vegetables that you may not be familiar with. I describe a few of them here.

Asian eggplant is long and thin, and is a vivid purple in color. The taste is lighter and less bitter than regular gourd-shaped black eggplant. It can be chopped without peeling and works well in mixed vegetable and rice dishes. I include it in several recipes.

Chayote is a pear-shaped green squash with a very mild taste, available in Mexican markets. I like to use it in pea soups and stews because it cooks to tenderness without falling apart.

Bottle gourd is available in Asian and Indian markets. It is green and shaped like a butternut squash. Like chayote, it is good in stews because it cooks to tenderness without falling apart.

Daikon is a large white radish, originally Asian, but I have seen it in regular supermarkets. It has a milder taste than little red radishes and can be used in similar ways in salads. It is also regularly used in miso soups and with other vegetables in Asian seasoned dishes.

Chinese Greens - if you have access to an Asian grocery with a decent produce department, you are in luck! There are several different tasty dark leafy greens you can find there that cook fairly quickly and taste wonderful. Look for Chinese broccoli, on choy, yu choy, bok choy, or Chinese cabbage, among others. Most of the ones I have tried have a decent refrigerated life span if kept dry in a closed plastic bag.

Care and Storage

These are recommendations for storage of vegetables for maximum usable life. I include notes where a vegetable could use a bit of extra care, or if my ideas are in conflict with what I see in most cookbooks I have seen.

Room temperature, in a relatively cool dry place out of the sun

- onions

- potatoes

- garlic

- apples

- winter squash (acorn, butternut) yams, sweet potatoes

Refrigerated, completely bagged in plastic

- celery. If you store celery in just the open-topped bag it usually comes in, it will be seriously wilted in 3-4 days. When you buy it, take a second plastic bag and double-bag it over the top so it is completely covered, and its fridge life is extended to something like 2 weeks.

- cabbage. This will keep indefinitely covered and refrigerated, which makes it a wonderful base for salads. If the outer edge or leaves get wilted or discolored, slice that part off and the rest is fine.

- leafy greens - Heavy greens like mustard greens, collards, kale, all keep at least a week, with collards and kale a bit longer. Lighter salad greens like spinach or salad mixes last 2-4 days. Lettuces seem to be the most fragile salad green. Greens keep best if they are bagged dry.

- root vegetables - carrots, turnips, beets, parsnips, radish and daikon(white radish). These seem to keep indefinitely if kept from drying out.

- scallions, parsley, cilantro. These are fragile and are past their peak in 3 days. Parsley and cilantro can be kept with their stems in a jar of water with the top bagged, which helps some. summer squash, zucchini, yellow squash, patty pan, chayote. These should be used within a week maximum, 3-4 days preferred. These can also be stored loosely bagged, so they get a little bit of air circulation. [2021 Update: I now usually use chopped sweet onion instead of scallions in salads since they have a much longer shelf life. I now very rarely buy these highly perishable vegetables.]

- salad greens and lettuces, and fresh spinach if dry and completely bagged, can keep up to 3-4 days maximum before they are soup greens at best. If the store where you buy them routinely showers their vegetables, especially lettuces like romaine, try to shake off as much of the water as you can before bagging. [2021 Update: Because of perishability I now concentrate on cabbage, kale, collards, and rarely buy these lighter greens.]

Some other vegetables like to breathe a bit, but partly covered. In a plastic bag they can get soft and moldy, but uncovered they dry out too quickly. These include

- ginger
- bell peppers and chilis.

Those vegetables I keep in a waxed paper bag in the fridge, or in a plastic bag that is loose and partly open.

The Problem of Fresh Greens

Getting enough good quality green leafy vegetables is a real problem when you do most of your shopping once a week and cook ahead a lot. Most leafy greens have relatively short shelf life, and salads made with spinach, lettuce or light salad greens can't be made in advance. For me living alone, I find that I can't work my way through a bag of fresh salad greens before they start to get wet, limp and icky.

It is also true that cooked greens do not reheat well.

There are a couple of ways to work around these problems.

You can plan to use the more perishable greens within a day or two of buying them fresh. If you shop on weekends, make Saturday, Sunday or Monday your fresh greens days, and plan meals that feature a fresh green salad or fresh cooked green dish.

Dense leafy greens like kale, collards, mustard greens and turnip greens can keep refrigerated uncooked for at least a week or longer, and they need to be cooked before eating. To save time, the greens can be washed and chopped up to a day in advance before cooking.

The Chinese greens I mentioned earlier in this chapter (on choy, bok choy, Chinese broccoli, napa cabbage) seem to keep up to a week if dry and bagged. These also need to be cooked.

The one green leafy vegetable I know of that has a long storage life, is good cooked or raw in salads, and works in salads prepared in advance, is common cabbage. Red or green cabbage are both good, with red cabbage having a stronger, slightly peppery flavor. Cabbage makes very good salads that can be eaten up to 3 or even 4 days after they are made. This makes them a good make-ahead side dish for dinners or lunches. I include several recipes with cabbage salads and cooked dishes do give ideas of how to prepare cabbage without getting monotonous.

Oils

Good quality oils can make a difference in the taste and quality of the food you cook. Some oils can get expensive, but they go a long way since you do not need to add a lot of oil to most dishes.

Some oils, like olive oil, are beststored in a cool dark place, or refrigerated, since they can go rancid. [Update 2021: Ghee and coconut oil seem to keep just fine at room temperature so I use them a lot.]

I like to have a couple of different oils around to vary the underlying taste of the food I cook.

Here are the ones I like to keep around.

Olive oil is my single favorite oil. You can usually find cold-pressed, extra virgin olive oil at decent prices, sometimes in half-gallon cans. Greek, Middle Eastern or Italian groceries are your best source for good buys on olive oil. By itself, it is the salad oil, and olive oil with garlic, salt and balsamic vinegar makes a wonderful dip for bread that sits lighter than butter.

You need to be careful with your cooking temperature when using olive oil. Olive oil has a low smoke point, so use a low-medium or low flame to cook with it by itself.

If I were going to keep only two oils around, I would use just olive oil and ghee or butter. Peanut oil would be my third.

Ghee, or clarified butter, has a higher smoke point than plain butter. It keeps indefinitely at room temperature. I use ghee when I want a distinct rich and buttery taste in food.

Peanut oil is a preferred oil used widely in Indian cooking. It also works well with rice or bean salads with savory herbs, and good peanut oil has a richer, denser taste than olive oil. [Update 2021: I realize many people have allergy issues with peanut oil; I am fortunate and can eat it. If you can't use peanut oil, **safflower oil** works well and behaves similarly.]

Sesame oil is commonly used in Oriental cooking, and is popular among people who are influenced by macrobiotic cooking. If you don't have sesame oil, peanut oil adds a nice flavor to Oriental cooking also. The most common kind of sesame oil in oriental markets is toasted and has a rich, dark brown color. It is used very sparingly as a condiment and adds a wonderful depth of flavor.

Invisible Seaweed

I am including seaweed, or sea vegetables, among suggested ingredients to have around. I realize that the idea of eating seaweed is hard to take for a lot of Americans. Here are some reasons why I suggest using them.

• They are a dried food that keeps indefinitely.

• They are used in small amounts, so they are economical.

• They are an excellent source of added minerals to your diet, including calcium, iron, and iodine.

• Correctly used they may increase the digestibility of beans, and enhance the flavor of beans, stews and other vegetables they are cooked with.

• They can be added invisibly to soups, salads and vegetable dishes, adding nutrition without being noticed.

That is why I call this section, Invisible Seaweed, using these wonderful sea vegetables without you or your guests noticing them. There are a few main kinds of sea vegetables that you may want to consider.

Kelp, sometimes called kombu, is a Japanese sea vegetable. It is a flat leaf, about the thickness of construction paper. It comes in small sheets, or cut up strips, or wrinkled sticks.

Kelp is used to cook with beans, in their cooking water, to make them easier to digest and to enhance their flavor. I use about a 3 inch stick of kelp (about 3" square if you have sheets) per cup of dried beans. Kelp also slightly thickens the cooking liquid for beans and stews. Cooked long enough, kombu just dissolves into the broth when stirred.

Kelp also has a natural flavor enhancing quality that works in the same way as msg, but without any negative side effects.

A slightly different variety of kelp is harvested from the Atlantic coast of North America.

Note that some health food stores sometimes carry ground kelp as a mineral supplement. This is not always the same plant as the whole kelp leaves, and can't be used in the same way.

Wakame is another Japanese seaweed that comes in dried sticks. It is soaked in cool water for 10 minutes or more and the soaking water is discarded. Wakame has soft thin leaves attached to a thicker stem that is cut away, and the leafy part can be chopped and added to soups, stews or salads. Wakame has a very mild flavor and soft texture that is masked by salty and sour seasoning.

All of these sea vegetables are available online or by mail order from Maine Coast Sea Vegetables, a company that harvests the Atlantic sea vegetables and sells them in bulk. You can find them online at, https:// seaveg.com/. Kelp and wakame are also available from some Asian markets, and in co-ops and stores that stock macrobiotic cooking ingredients.

On Using Chilis

There are a wide variety of chili peppers available, both fresh and dried, used in cooking around the world, and they are very popular in much vegetarian cooking, especially Indian and Mexican. (If you are interested in cooking with chilis, my favorite site is, Chili Pepper Madness - https://www.chilipeppermadness.com/ .)

Here is a list of some of the chilis commonly available, listed roughly in order of hotness.

Fresh Chilis

- Green and red bell pepper
- Anaheim
- Poblano
- Jalapeno
- Serrano
- Asian small chilis
- Habanero

Dried Chilis

- Ancho

- New Mexico

- Guajillo

- Chipotle (smoky)

- Arbol, most small thin chilis

- dried Habanero, ghost peppers, carolina reapers. If you know peppers well enough to use these extra-hot varieties you don't need my advice. If you are new to hot peppers leave these extra hots alone.

Almost all of the chilis in this list are available in Mexican markets, and in some regular supermarkets.

Oriental, Indian and Middle Eastern stores stock small whole dried red chilis which are quite hot. Oriental stores also have jars of hot chili with vinegar and salt, which makes a good table condiment.

Ground chili powder in Oriental and Middle Eastern markets is just dried ground red chilis. This is not the same as the spice mix called chili powder found in American markets. I suggest using the whole dried chilis rather than the powder because the taste is usually fresher. You can grind your own chili powder in an electric coffee grinder (probably not the same one you grind coffee in).

The dried guajillo chili, which is very flavorful and not very hot, is the one I use most often. I take the dried chili, remove the seeds and stems and cut it up into small, fingernail-size pieces with a scissors, and use the pieces sauteed in hot oil in the first step of cooking to let the flavor permeate the oil. I keep a little jar of cut up guajillo chili pieces ready to go.

The smaller dried red chilis, available in Asian, Indian and Middle Eastern groceries, are often quite a bit hotter. To add flavor with them while minimizing heat, use the dried chili whole, adding it to the hot oil early as usual. You can also cut up the chili and discard the stems and seeds, although this will be hotter than leaving the whole chili.

Whichever kind of chili you use, discarding the seeds cuts down on the hotness of the chili and keeps much of the flavor. Despite their formidable reputation, jalapenos are hardly hot at all without their seeds, and serranos without their seeds are usually medium hot.

Whenever you work with chilis, wash your hands well afterwards with warm soapy water because the chili oil can irritate the skin. Make sure not to touch around your eyes while working with chilis. Some people recommend wearing gloves while working with the very hot chilis, although I have not found that to be necessary for the ones I list here.

For the recipes in this book that call for either fresh or dried chilis, you can use different ones according to what is available to you, taking into account that you may need to adjust amounts to get the desired level of taste and hotness.

Convenience Foods and Condiments

These are some convenience foods and seasonings I like to keep around.

- Tofu

- Canned Beans, peas, corn

- Soy Sauce

- Fish Sauce

- Toasted Sesame Oil

- Gochujang

- Vinegar (Plain, Wine)

- Lemon juice

- Honey and/or maple syrup

- Sugar, brown sugar

Tofu is fermented soybean curd. It comes in soft white blocks. Tofu is soft, bland and easy to digest, and it combines well with other foods. Chopped and mashed and cooked with other foods, it takes on the texture of scrambled eggs. It can also be blended with oil and seasonings to make good creamy dips and sauces. It is available fresh in tubs of water, or in anaeobic packages that I prefer, which keep indefinitely without refrigeration.

The kind of tofu you use makes a big difference in texture. My personal favorite is Mori-Nu Silken tofu which comes in shelf stable containers that store indefinitely without refrigeration. The tofu I find refrigerated in water at most groceries does not have the extremely smooth texture of Mori-Nu; its texture is a bit more grainy.

Canned beans are useful to have around for quick dinners. It is a good idea to drain and rinse canned beans before cooking, especially if cooking a relatively dry dish, so I don't recommend buying beans in prepared sauces. Regular supermarkets usually have canned kidneys, pintos. black beans and chickpeas. Middle Eastern stores have fava beans, which are very good sauteed with onion, garlic and spices. Mexican stores carry canned pinto and black beans. If you prefer organic, there are a few different brands available in co-ops and some stores, some of them with the beans cooked with the seaweed kombu for digestibility.

Soy milk and rice milk, or blends, or milks made from nuts or oats, are good light substitutes for milk in cooking. Almond milk is my current personal favorite. Some of them are available in anaerobic packages that do not need refrigeration until opened.

Wheat gluten or Seitan, also called mock duck, mock chicken or mock whatever, is a chewy, meat-textured product made from the gluten of wheat. It is available in small cans at Asian groceries, or in the Oriental section of some large supermarkets. Some natural food stores carry more expensive brands that I find inferior in taste and texture to the inexpensive canned product. It is good cooked with vegetables or rice to provide the dense and chewy texture of meat.

[2021 Update: mock duck is now much more expensive so I rarely use it. It might be worth checking out if you crave foods with the chewiness of meat.]

Frozen vegetables such as corn and peas are useful to have around for occasional salads and quick meals. Frozen spinach is good in dips. It is now common to find other dark leafy vegetables like kale and collard greens available frozen.

Miso is a fermented soybean paste, widely available at Oriental markets and at some co-ops and natural food stores. It has a strong, salty-sour taste, and is commonly used in the far east as the main flavoring for clear broth vegetable soups. It also works well in strong tasting gravies. I include recipes for miso soup, and for a miso-onion gravy.

Soy sauce, also called shoyu or tamari, is a primary seasoning in many Oriental spice patterns. With good, naturally fermented soy sauce, the ingredient list should be limited to: soybeans, water, sometimes wheat, and salt, sometimes with a preservative added. Avoid inferior soy sauce that includes corn syrup or artificial coloring or flavoring. [2021 Update: The world is catching up with my taste - the generic house brand at my supermarket is now Kikkoman quality and is much less expensive.]

Fish sauce is made from fermented anchovies and salt. It has a strong smell that takes some getting used to, but the taste is very addicting. It is now one of my favorite salty condiments. I use Squid Brand, which is the most widely available and the least expensive, and I think is one of the consistently best tasting. (Yes, I know this is not strictly vegetarian, but it is such a wonderful taste addition to the cuisine that I include it here.)

Toasted Sesame Oil is available at Asian markets. It has a rich smoky taste and is used in tiny amounts as a condiment.

Gochujang is a Korean hot and slightly sweet fermented bean paste. It's a hot Korean variant of miso.

Basic Recipe Patterns - Frameworks for Creativity

If you use many cookbooks at all - which I have, over the past 50 plus years of cooking - you will start to notice that even cookbooks that look like they have hundreds of recipes, actually have only a handful of recipe patterns, with some variants on the ingredients. Once you really understand a recipe pattern, you have the ability to take similar ingredients and come up with your own individual variants, your own recipes. Do enough cooking and you will come up with your own personal cook's instinct, that guides you to what mix of ingredients and spices feels right for this particular meal. That's where you start really being a vegetarian cook.

For those of you who knit and are Elizabeth Zimmerman fans, a recipe is like her 'Blind Follower' directions where every stitch and row is spelled out, and a recipe pattern is like her usual instructions, where she explains the construction of a garment clearly enough that you can create variations of your own.

In this section I cover the recipe patterns that I find myself using day in and day out. These are the underlying patterns on which the sample recipes are based. Master these, and you can run with them and improvise your own specific meals. Also, you never need to exactly repeat a dish, so that even the same recipe, with the same ingredients, will come out a bit different each time.

Basic Rice And Veggies Recipe Pattern

This is an outline of the steps involved in those recipes that involve a grain mixed and cooked with sauteed vegetables and spices.

Preliminary Step: Choose Grain, Spice Pattern and Main Ingredients The main categories of ingredients are

- the grain

- the spice pattern

- the oil

- main vegetables

   - complement (bean, mock duck, or tofu. Note that mock duck complements texture but does not provide protein complementarity.)

   - garnishes (nuts, light greens)

Step One: Heat the Oil

Turn the flame under your skillet to a comfortable medium-low heat, add the oil and let it heat a bit before adding anything else. Avoid heating the oil to smoke point.

Step Two (Optional): First Group of Condiments

Add the condiments that you want to pre-cook in the oil. These include brown mustard seeds or cumin seeds, and dried or fresh chilies. Garlic and ginger also go in at this step, right after the seeds if you use them.

Step Three: Chop and add Veggies, Salt and Spices

If I am using onions they always go in before the other main veggies, and I saute them until they are starting to turn transparent before adding anything else. I add salt and spices at this step and stir before adding anything else.

I like to add condiment veggies like celery or bell peppers next so their taste permeates the oil.

76

Next come slower cooking root vegetables like potatoes or carrots. If I am making a wet dish, I add water or canned diced tomatoes after the root vegetables are in to help their cooking. Slow cooking root vegetables like potatoes need a low flame and occasional stirring to cook through without burning.

Near the end of cooking time I add quick cooking vegetables like zucchini, eggplant or mushrooms.

Step Four (Optional): Add the Complement

This can be cooked beans, or tofu, tempeh or mock duck. I usually add the complement when most of the vegetables are pretty much cooked, usually around the same time as the quick cooking vegetables. Stir thoroughly and get them completely heated through.

Step Five (Optional): Stir in the Rice or Other Grain and Heat

You can stir your cooked rice or grain in with the cooked veggies at this point. Or, you can keep the two separate and serve the veggies to be spooned over the rice as a sauce or stew.

Step Six (Optional): Final Condiments and Garnishes

At the very end, just before serving, is when I add the final garnishes, stirring them in right before carrying the dish to the table to serve. These include parsley or cilantro, or scallions. Nuts or seeds are last-minute additions also.

If I am going to use lemon juice or vinegar, I add them near the end also. With Oriental cooking I usually add the soy sauce near the end, after the rice is in, since good quality soy sauce has nutrients that are lost with long cooking. Let the dish sit on a very low flame for 3 to 5 minutes to let the flavors blend before adding your final garnish and serving.

Example Grain and Vegetables Recipes

Variations:

- Basic Veggies and Beans - follow rice and veggies pattern and omit the rice. Serve with rice or bread on the side.

Example Vegetable and Beans Recipe

All Purpose Rice (Grain) Salad Pattern

Since rice or other grain salad is such a useful dish to know how to make, and how to keep interesting, I want to discuss the different parts of a grain salad, to give you variations to choose from. A grain salad consists of a combination of the following.

- dressing

- grain

- other garnishes

- vegetables

- bean (optional)

(seeds, nuts, grated cheese)

Basic Salad Dressings

Salad dressing is a mixture of oil + salty + sour + spices, and varying the various parts of the mix can make a big difference in taste. Here are some of my favorite combinations to get you started experimenting on your own.

Salad Oils include Olive (my favorite), peanut, safflower, sesame, smoked sesame.

Salty taste can be plain salt, or soy sauce, fish sauce, or something pickled like olives, or kimchi, or dill pickles.

Sour can be some kind of vinegar (plain, wine, apple cider, balsamic) or lemon juice.

Seasonings... you name it. I commonly use pepper (red or black), garlic, onion or scallion, basil, parsley, cilantro, oregano, ginger, dill.

Vegetables - choose any combination of the following - 3 to 4 vegetables is usually a good number. I almost always include scallions and either parsley or cilantro. [Update note: I now usually use chopped sweet onions since scallions have a very limited shelf life before they wilt. If the onions are too sharp you can take the edge off by slicing them and letting them sit in iced water for an hour.]

- scallions or yellow sweet onions

- radish, white or red, grated

- sugar snap peas, steamed

- parsley or cilantro

- grated carrot

- snow peas, steamed

- cherry tomatoes

- zucchini, grated or chopped

- frozen peas or corn, thawed, or canned

- red or green bell peppers

- chopped celery

- cucumber

Grain - Short grain white rice is my favorite for a substantial and versatile salad. Short grain brown rice makes a heavier, denser, softer salad. Long grain rice makes a lighter salad. Bulghur (cracked wheat) is the main grain in tabouli. And of course there's pasta, or pasta plus rice, or wild rice mixed in with another rice, or...use your imagination.

Bean - Pintos, kidneys, small red beans, black beans, all work well with rice. Lentils and chickpeas work well with rice or bulghur. Any of those beans work with pasta. Beans make a salad heavier and much more substantial, and they lend themselves to stronger seasoning. I suggest a proportion of grain to beans in a salad around 3 or 4 to 1.

Other garnishes - sesame or sunflower seeds, or chopped nuts like walnuts or almonds, or a flavorful cheese like feta or parmesan, can vary a salad.

Perking Up Leftover Salad - When I make a salad to use for 3 or 4 days for lunch, I find it helpful to increase the sour or salty taste after the first 2 days, and/or add a new garnish to keep it interesting. A leftover grain and vegetable salad can always be heated up with a little extra oil and spice to make a hot main dish.

Sample Grain Salad Recipe:

Rice and Vegetable Salad Sample   73

Basic Bean Stew or Dal Recipe Pattern

This is an outline of the steps involved in those recipes that involve a bean with its cooking liquid as the base of a stew or soup, mixed and cooked with sauteed vegetables and spices.

Preliminary Step: Choose Bean, Spice Pattern and Vegetables The main categories of ingredients are

- the bean

- the spice pattern

- the oil

- main vegetables

- garnishes (nuts, light greens)

Preliminary: Presoak bean if necessary

Step One: Cook beans in water plus supporting spices. For me this usually involves adding kombu and turmeric, and sometimes ginger and fennel. When the beans are done, add salt.

Step Two: (Optional) Add (some)Vegetables. Diced tomatoes go in at this step, along with vegetables like potatoes, beets, parsnips or longer cooking squash, that you do not want sauteed first. Cook until vegetables are done. The saute step can be done while the root vegetables are cooking.

Step Three: the Saute. With the next steps, the same principles apply as in the Rice and

Vegetables pattern. They are:

- Heat the Oil

- (Optional) First Group of Condiments

- Chop and add Veggies, Salt and Spices

Step Four: Add Sauteed Veggies to the Cooked Beans

If possible, give the stew with the sauteed veggies at least 15 to 30 minutes for the flavors to blend.

Step Six (Optional): Final Condiments and Garnishes

The same principles apply here as in the garnish step for Rice and Veggies.

Sample Bean Recipes

- Greek Split Pea Soup 60
- Simple Blackeyed Peas   62
- Black Bean Chili   66

Spice and Condiment Patterns - the Key to Variety of Taste

What I want to cover in this section of the book are spice patterns, groups of spices and condiments that work well together. They are grouped this way so that, in planning a recipe, you can choose from among the spices in a group and be fairly sure that they will work. This provides a framework within which you can learn to improvise your cooking.

Within each group, I have the condiments I consider essential listed first, with other supporting condiments listed for variety. When you are just starting to stock your spice pantry, you can concentrate on the essential spices first, and venture into the complementary lists as time, budget and inclination allows.

I also list the oils that go well with each condiment type, and I include condiment vegetables like garlic and ginger, and traditional prepared seasonings like soy sauce in these groups.

Please note that I do not pretend to be an expert on Indian, Oriental, Mediterranean or Mexican cooking. This is a low-budget American Eclectic vegetarian cook's labels for groups of spices that I find work well together.

Basic Plain Condiments

- these go with most everything

- salt
- pepper
- garlic
- ginger
- lemon juice

- dill

- onion, raw or sauteed

Pretty much all of the flavors in this group blend in with any of the other spice patterns. The one exception is dill, which is distinct enough to stand on its own in some salads and dips.

Olive oil is my favorite. It will work with any of the spice patterns I mention here. [Update: I now sometimes use coconut oil, which has a high smoke point. It works well in hot dishes but not salads.]

When I use butter in cooking for flavor, I sometimes combine it with either safflower or peanut oil. I sometimes use ghee instead of butter.

I include onion as a basic spice since I use it very often as a base flavor. Sauteed onion serves to bind flavors in a dish together. Sauteed slowly and long at a low temperature, onions can get quite sweet and buttery tasting. Sauteed more quickly, or until slightly browned, they give a dish a little bit more of an edge.

Chopped garlic and ginger are condiments I usually add fairly early on to hot oil, before onions and other vegetables. I very highly recommend using good fresh ginger root and garlic in your cooking. It makes a world of difference. If you can't find fresh ginger, dried ginger powder makes a poor substitute. Some Middle Eastern and Indian stores also sell a ginger paste and a garlic paste that are adequate. If you use the pastes, take into account that they have salt and vinegar added, and adjust your spices accordingly.

In this basic group, and in most of the other groups, I include sour condiments like lemon juice or vinegar. I find that using a little bit of a good sour taste lets me cut down on the amount of salt I use. It complements and 'sharpens' the salt taste.

Using lemon juice in recipes, use fresh lemons when you can, as the taste difference is noticeable. There is a good brand of unprocessed organic lemon juice available at coops and some large supermarkets. If you can't find those, your usual 'reconstituted' lemon juice in a bottle is adequate.

Recipes using Basic Spice Pattern

Indian - the Usual Spices

Essential

- turmeric

- cumin

- coriander

- ginger

- dried chilis

Supporting

- bay leaf

- brown mustard seeds

- fennel

Oils

- ghee or butter

- peanut or safflower

This section is named from instructions I saw on a prepared mix for a chickpea-tomato dish I like, which said to cook the chickpeas "with the usual spices".

Turmeric, ground coriander and ground cumin go beautifully together and serve as a subtle flavor base that can be varied with the supporting spices or stand on its own. Also, turmeric cooked with beans aids with their digestion.

Brown mustard seeds are added whole to hot oil, before other ingredients. The raw seeds are pungent, but cooked in the oil they turn mild and have a subtle toasted nutty flavor. Cook them in the oil until they turn black and begin to pop and spatter - it's a good idea to have a cover on your skillet when you use them. Once they are spattering, add the next ingredients - ginger and garlic if you are using them, then the onion.

Cumin seeds when used whole can also be added to the hot oil at the same time as mustard seeds and before anything else. They are greyish brown in color. Cook them until they turn a more definite brown.

If you are interested in seriously exploring Indian vegetarian cooking, I recommend the book, *Lord Krishna's Cuisine* by Yamuna Devi.

Recipes using 'The Usual' Indian Spices

Warming Spices

- allspice
- cloves
- black pepper
- cinnamon
- nutmeg
- ground cardamom

In Indian cooking, "garam masala" means warming spices, and this is a list of some of the common ingredients in that spice mixture.. It goes well with The Usual Indian Spices listed above to give food an aromatic spiciness. Indian curry powder is a prepackaged blend of ground spices largely from these two lists.

In European cooking, this same pungent spice group is pumpkin pie spice, hot mulled wine spice, hot cereal spice. It goes well with hot cereals with apples, raisins and nuts, or with sweet vegetables like squash or yams. They work well with a sweet ingredient in the main flavor. They oils they work well with are nutty, buttery or sweet, like peanut oil, corn oil or butter.

Some variant on this pungent spice pattern also gives the distinctive flavor to chai, or spiced tea.

Recipes Using Warming Spices

Mediterranean

- basil
- marjoram
- olive oil
- oregano
- thyme
- lemon juice
- bay leaf
- mint
- red wine vinegar
- balsamic vinegar

This is your basic pizza sauce or spaghetti sauce type spice pattern. They are used in Italian, Greek, and other Mediterranean cooking. They are often used in tomato sauces, and they work well with sauteed beans with garlic, onion and bell peppers. They can also give an Italian or Greek flavor to a salad.

This group also works well with the Savory spice group.

Recipes Using Mediterranean Spices

- Bulghur with Vegetables   56
- Greek Split Pea Soup 60
- Red Lentil Soup   61
- Mediterranean Beans and Vegetables   67
- Tabouli Salad 74
- Spicy Cabbage Salad 76
- Oven Roasted Vegetables   80
- Serious Tomato Sauce   84
- Spaghetti and Mock Duck with (or without) Tomato Sauce 85
- Quinoa Patties   58
- Rice and Bulghur with Vegetables   57

Savory Spices

Main Spices	**Supporting Spices**
• Rosemary	• nutmeg
• Sage	• marjoram
• Parsley (often dried)	• basil
• Thyme	• bay leaf
• Black Pepper	

This group of spices is also known as 'poultry seasoning' and is associated with the taste of thanksgiving turkey stuffing. They go wonderfully together with a variety of rice and bean hot dishes and salads. These spices also work well with the Mediterranean group.

Recipes Using Savory Spices

Yellow Split Pea Soup 60

Lentil Stew   63

Simple Blackeyed Peas   62

Chickpea Rice Salad 74

Creamy Parsnip Oat Soup   82

Vegetable Tomato Barley Soup   83

Onion Miso Gravy   86

Quinoa Casserole   59

Oriental/Asian Spices

Main Condiments

- soy sauce
- fish sauce
- rice or wine vinegar
- chilis

Supporting

- basil
- chinese five spice
- sugar

Oils and other

- sesame oil
- smoked sesame oil (more like a condiment)
- miso
- black bean garlic sauce
- other bean based sauces like gochujang

When I am using a soy sauce with or without a vinegar, I sometimes add just a little bit of sugar to the dish. It takes the edge off of the salty soy sauce taste and makes the dish a bit more rounded and satisfying. Soy sauce works best used to support and enhance the flavors of food rather than as a foreground salty taste.

Fish sauce has become one of my favorite salty condiments, and I will often use just fish sauce, chilis and vinegar as seasoning.

Chinese five spice is a blend of ground spices with an aromatic, anise-like tone. Use it very sparingly; if you try to add enough, you probably used too much.

Miso is a fermented soybean paste with a distinctive salty and sour taste. It is commonly used in soups, and can also be used to flavor sauces.

Black bean garlic sauce, a variant of miso, is pretty widely available in jars in Asian groceries, and is a strong distinct sauce base in its own right.

Gochujang is a Korean paste based on fermented beans plus sugar and chilis. It's kind of like miso with an attitude.

Recipes Using Oriental Spices

Mexican Spices

- fresh chilis
- dried chilis
- smoked chilis
- roasted chilis
- cumin
- oregano
- garlic
- epazote
- did I mention chilis?

Dried ground red chilis, ranging from mild to insanely hot, form the distinctive spice base for the dish called chili, along with ground cumin, oregano and garlic, and chilis of various sorts form the base for a lot of Mexican cooking.

Epazote is an herb, available dried in Mexican markets, that gives a distinctive taste to black bean soups.

Recipes Using Mexican Spices

Sample Recipes

Notes on the Recipes

In all of these recipes, spice amounts are approximate, so vary them according to your taste. For the most part I have gone light on the spices and salt. You can always add more, but you can't add less once they are in.

All spices are dried except when noted.

Bean amounts - 1 cup dried beans yields about 2 ½ cups cooked beans. 1 can of canned beans drained and rinsed usually yields about 1 ½ cups cooked beans.

Doubling a recipe - you can safely double all ingredients except the spices, which will intensify. Try about 1 ½ times the spice amounts and adjust from there.

Slow cookers intensify spices, so you may want to try using less if you are adapting a stovetop recipe.

Using the spice patterns - for most of the recipes that I identify a spice pattern, you can experiment with varying the spices by using others from the same group.

Cooking time will vary according to a lot of factors - your stove or oven, your cookware, how high a flame you use, how old your beans are, time of year and weather, and so on. It takes time to get used to a new stove or new cookware. Allow a 25% fudge factor on cooking time until you get to know your equipment and cooking style.

If you use an **electric stove**, take into account that the burners cannot adjust temperature rapidly, so you need to be more careful to avoid scorching. When cooking grains you may want to bring the grain and water to a boil on one burner, then transfer it to another burner preheated to the low steeping temperature. If you use a flame tamer, pre heat that on the burner also.

Grain Recipes

Rice and Vegetables with Diced Tomatoes

Spice pattern - 'The Usual' Indian

The brown mustard seeds, cumin seeds and garlic are the dominant spice flavors in this dish. I cook the celery in with the onion to use it like a spice. The pat of butter isn't necessary, but makes the dish just a little bit richer. For variation, you could add other vegetables like bell peppers or grated carrot.

1 c short grain white rice	salt and pepper to taste
1½ c water	1 medium onion, chopped
½ tsp salt	1 stalk celery, chopped
¼ tsp turmeric	1 zucchini chopped
Peanut or sesame oil	1 small can diced tomatoes

1 pat butter (optional) or ghee (or you can use just ghee)

1/2 tsp whole brown mustard seeds

1/2 tsp whole cumin seeds

2 cloves garlic, chopped

Cook the short grain rice as usual with turmeric added, or use leftover rice.

While the rice is cooking, heat the oil and butter or ghee in a skillet on a medium flame. When the butter is thoroughly melted, add the brown mustard and cumin seeds and cover. When the mustard seeds start to pop and spatter, add the garlic, cover again and let cook another minute. Add onion and celery, stir and cook until onion starts to turn transparent. Add the zucchini, stir, and cook until zucchini is desired softness. Add diced tomatoes, stir, and heat until thoroughly hot. Stir in the cooked rice and cook for 3 minutes to blend flavors. (If using leftover cold rice, heat until thoroughly hot, stirring occasionally.) You can serve immediately, or keep in a covered dish in a 200 degree oven until ready to serve.

Rice and Vegetables 'Mexicano'

Spice pattern - Mexican

The dried guajillo chili gives the distinctive flavor to this dish. Guajillo is only mildly hot, so if you substitute the skin of another dried chili you may want to adjust the amount depending on your heat tolerance. Or, you can use chili flakes or powder.

If you use eggplant you will need more oil, since eggplant soaks it up.

The recipe calls for ground cumin, but you could add whole cumin seeds to the hot oil with the chilis for a more vivid flavor.

2-4 tbsp olive oil

salt to taste

1 Asian eggplant or 1 small regular eggplant, chopped (optional)

1 tsp guajillo chili, cut up

2 cloves garlic

1 medium onion, chopped

3 c cooked white or brown rice

1 stalk celery, chopped

½ tsp oregano

1 tbsp lime or lemon juice

½ tsp ground cumin

scallions or parsley or cilantro to garnish

Saute the chili skins in the oil as it heats. Add garlic and saute another minute, then add the onion, celery and spices and saute until onion is transparent. Add eggplant and saute until eggplant is desired level of doneness. When the vegetables are thoroughly done, stir in the cooked rice and heat up. Just before serving, add the lime juice and stir, then stir in the garnish.

Variations:

Saute bell peppers or anaheim peppers with the vegetables.

Add a small can of diced tomatoes for a wetter dish.

Rice with Pinto Beans and Vegetables

Spice Pattern: Oriental

I like to use the long, thin purple eggplant in this dish since they don't need peeling. If you use the large eggplant, try it with and without the skins and see which you prefer. The dish also works well without the eggplant.

3 tbsp peanut and canola oil

2 tsp chopped ginger

2 cups cooked pinto beans, or 1 can pinto beans, rinsed and drained

1 med onion chopped

1 bell pepper or anaheim chili, chopped

1 small eggplant, chopped (optional)

1 stalk celery chopped

¼ tsp turmeric

½-1 tsp dried basil

1 small can diced tomatoes

2 cloves garlic

3 c cooked rice

1-2 tbsp soy sauce or to taste

1 tbsp red wine vinegar or to taste

Saute the ginger and garlic in the oil. Add onion and saute until transparent. Add bell peppers and eggplant and saute until peppers start to get soft. Add tomatoes and heat, then add the pintos and heat. Add rice and heat. When hot all the way through, add the soy sauce and red wine vinegar and heat another 2-3 min. Serve

Variation: omit soy sauce and vinegar, and add either savory or Mediterranean spices with lemon juice.

Variation: other vegetables like zucchini or grated carrot work well also.

99

Afghani Basmati Rice with Raisins and Carrots

Spice pattern: Warming

This is my version of a fabulous rice dish served at the Crescent Moon Bakery, an Afghani restaurant near where I live. Theirs is better. I am giving a range of oil and butter amount that you can adjust to your taste and preference. You don't need to include all of the spices listed, and you can vary amounts to adjust to your taste.

1 c basmati rice	1½ c water	½ tsp salt
1 pat butter or 1-2 tsp olive oil		

2 tbsp olive oil	1-2 tbsp butter	¼ c raisins
1/2 c warm water (to soak the raisins)		1 carrot, grated
salt to taste	1/8 tsp allspice	
1/8 tsp black pepper	1/8 tsp cardamom	

Cook the basmati rice, either stovetop or steamed, with or without the butter. While the rice is cooking, saute the other ingredients in the oil on a low flame. When the rice is cooked, either stir the rice in with the oil spice mix, or serve the rice topped with the mix.

Variation: cook the raisins in with the rice instead of sauteing them with the vegetables. This will make the sweetness more gentle and more pervasive. Increase the cooking water by ¼ cup. You can also add ¼ tsp turmeric to the rice, which will give it a bright yellow color.

White Rice and Moong Dal

Spice pattern: 'The Usual' Indian

You can leave out the split peas and adjust the water accordingly and have a spiced cooked rice.

1 tbsp peanut or canola oil

1/2 tsp whole cumin seeds

1/2 tsp chopped ginger

1 tbsp butter

1/2 tsp fennel seeds

2 c white rice, short or long grain

1/3 c moong dal, washed and rinsed

> or 1/3 c yellow split peas, washed and rinsed

¼ tsp turmeric

½ tsp salt or to taste

3 ½ c boiling water

Parsley or cilantro to garnish (optional)

Soak the moong dal or split peas at least 3 hours in cold water, and drain.

In your rice cooking pot, saute the seeds and ginger in the oil for a few minutes until the cumin seeds change color to a richer brown. Add the rice, peas and seasoning, stir and saute for 1-2 minutes. Add the boiling water, stir and bring back to a boil. Cover and cook for about 25 minutes, then let sit for another 10 minutes. Stir and serve, with or without the garnish.

Linguine with Spinach

Spice pattern: Basic

This recipe works as well with fresh chard, chopped with the stems removed.

1 lb linguine or egg noodles. cooked according to package directions

4 tbsp olive oil

½-1 tsp basil

3 cloves garlic

salt and pepper to taste

1 package frozen chopped spinach, or 8-10 oz fresh chopped spinach

½ c chopped walnuts

1-2 tbsp balsamic vinegar

While the linguine is cooking, saute the garlic in the olive oil until starting to brown. Add the spices, spinach and walnuts and cook over a low flame. When the linguine is done, toss with the spinach and add the balsamic vinegar. Serve

Variation: Grated parmesan cheese makes a nice garnish.

Soba Noodles and Vegetables

Spice pattern: Oriental

Soba noodles are a Japanese buckwheat noodle. While the soba adds a distinctive roasted nutty grain taste, this dish also works with egg noodles or spaghetti. I suggest going light on the soy sauce and vinegar to let the sauteed veggie taste come through.

If you omit the soy sauce and vinegar and increase the butter, you get a dish that has a buttered pasta with veggies taste that is also very good.

8 oz soba or other noodles

2 tbsp peanut oil	1 pat butter (optional)
2 cloves garlic	¼ tsp dried red chilis
or 1-2 tsp finely chopped ginger	
1 med onion chopped	1 zucchini chopped
1-2 tbsp soy sauce	1 tbsp red wine vinegar
black pepper to taste	

chopped scallions to garnish - optional

Cook the noodles according to package directions. While the noodles are cooking, saute the garlic, onion and chilis until onions are transparent. Add the zucchini and cook until tender, about 4-5 min. Add the cooked pasta and remaining seasonings, stir and serve.

Noodles with Mock Duck and Onions

Spice pattern: Basic or Oriental

This is a noodles and veggies dish where the distinctive taste comes from the large amount of cooked onions. Start the onions going while the pasta water is heating and cook them at least 15 minutes over a low flame for a sweet, rich buttery taste. Go light on the other spices to let the onions dominate.

1 lb spaghetti, egg noodles or soba noodles

4 tbsp peanut oil

(or 2 tbsp peanut oil and 2 tbsp butter)

1-2 cloves garlic

½ tsp ginger chopped

3-4 med onions chopped

or 2 large onions chopped

salt and pepper to taste

(or soy sauce, pepper and wine vinegar to taste)

1 small can wheat gluten, drained and chopped

Cook the noodles according to package directions. While the noodles are cooking, saute the ginger, garlic and onion with the salt and pepper on a low flame for as long as you can. Add the mock duck about 4 min before the noodles are done. Add the cooked pasta, adjust seasoning and serve.

Spaghetti with Ketchup

Spice pattern: Neo-Brooklyn

This tastes great, and it's a good dish to cook for one when you don't want to open a whole can or jar of tomato sauce.

Gochujang is a Korean hot bean paste condiment. You can find it in Korean and some Asian groceries, and it is available online.

Spaghetti

Ketchup - 2-3 Splortches or to taste

1 tsp Gochujang (optional) or other Hot Sauce if desired

1/2 to 1 tsp toasted sesame oil (optional, but man, does it add flavor!)

garlic

onion

bell or hot peppers

oil for the veggies - I use olive or peanut

Cook the pasta according to package directions. While that is cooking, saute the vegetables in oil.

Stir the cooked pasta in with the vegetables, add the ketchup, gochujang and sesame oil. Mix well, and let it fry a bit longer to let the tastes cook in.

NOTE: If you're too highfalutin to be caught dead cooking with ketchup, consider substituting a mix of tomato sauce, a bit of honey or sugar, and some vinegar - a tomato taste that is sharp, salty and a bit sweet - you know, like ketchup.

Spicy Cream of Wheat

Spice pattern - 'The Usual' Indian spices plus some warming spice.

This can be done as a sweet and spicy breakfast cereal, or as a grain side dish at dinner. You could add any of the other warming spices (cinnamon, cloves, nutmeg, black pepper) as desired. If you want the raisin taste to be more vivid, you can soak the raisins in very warm water for at least 15 min and then use the raisins and soaking water in the recipe, counting the soaking water as part of the total cooking water.

2 c cold water	1/2 c raisins
½ c peanuts or other nuts	1 apple, chopped (optional)
¼ tsp turmeric	1/4 tsp ground coriander
¼ tsp ground cumin	pinch of allspice
1 pat butter	
salt to taste (½ - 1 tsp)	honey to taste (start with 1 tbsp)
½ c cream of wheat	

Proportion of water to grain is 4:1

Add the water, raisins and peanuts to your pot and start the water heating while you add all the other ingredients except the cream of wheat. When the water is at full boil, add the cream of wheat slowly while stirring. Reduce to low flame and cook for 3-4 minutes until the wheat thickens, stirring most of the time. Serve with soymilk as a breakfast cereal.

Variation: Keep the same seasonings and use steel cut oats - 4:1 water to grain, 30 minutes stovetop, 45 minutes to an hour baked at 375 degrees. No stirring is needed with the oats until cooking is done.

Bulghur with Vegetables

Spice pattern: basic or Mediterranean

A good, quick one-dish meal. It makes a good 'MustGo' dinner where you vary the vegetables according to what's in the fridge. Varying the spice pattern, the mix of vegetables, or the oil used, is enough to keep this simple dish interesting. Most of the ingredients are marked optional just to give you an idea of the range of vegetables or spices you can include or exclude to vary the taste and texture.

1 c bulghur   2 c water   ½ tsp salt   ½ tsp black pepper

½ tsp basil (optional)   ½ tsp oregano (optional)

2-4 tbsp olive or peanut oil   and/or butter

1 med onion chopped   1 bell pepper chopped (optional)

1 tsp chopped ginger (optional)

2-3 cloves garlic   1 stalk celery chopped

1 carrot grated (optional)   1 zucchini chopped (optional)

1-2 tbsp lemon juice   (or red wine vinegar for a sharper taste)

1 c cooked chickpeas (optional)

Cook the bulghur in the water with salt until done, about 15 minutes. While the bulghur is cooking, saute the ginger, garlic, onions and spices, (and bell pepper) in the oil until onions and pepper are desired softness. Add the other vegetables and cook to desired doneness. Stir in the bulghur, adjust salt, and lemon juice and cook another 5 minutes. Serve.

Variation: Omit the oregano and use some of the savory spices instead (rosemary, thyme, sage, nutmeg).

Mediterranean Rice with Chickpeas: Cook up 1 c rice of your choice, and use the rice instead of the bulghur.

Rice and Bulghur with Vegetables

Spice Pattern: Mediterranean

This dish takes its special taste and texture from the mix of bulghur with white rice. The two grains complement each other and make the dish surprisingly different from either grain by itself.

3 tbsp olive oil 1 zucchini chopped   2 tsp chopped ginger

1 purple eggplant chopped (optional)

2 cloves garlic chopped   1 small can diced tomatoes

1 large onion chopped   1 green bell pepper chopped

1 c cooked white rice   1 c cooked bulghur

½ tsp salt or to taste   ½ tsp pepper

1 tsp basil   1 tbsp lemon juice   1 tsp oregano

Saute the ginger and garlic in the heated oil until they just start to brown, then add the onions, bell peppers and spices, and cook until vegetables are soft. Add zucchini and eggplant, stir and cook until they soften. Add diced tomatoes and heat through, then add the rice and bulghur and heat through. Add lemon juice, adjust seasoning, cook another 5 minutes and serve.

Variation: The dish is moist, so I sometimes cook it about a half an hour in advance and then keep it warm in a covered pyrex dish in a 275 degree oven. That extra time seems to let the flavors blend a bit more.

The dish texture changes if you vary proportion of the grains. I like 2:1 rice to bulghur. I'm not sure if it would work with more bulghur than rice.

Baked Steel Cut Oats with Raisins and Peanuts

Spice pattern: warming

Use McCann's Irish Steel-cut Oats if you can find them. Steel cut oats are much denser and heavier than rolled oats.

1 c steel cut oats (McCann's preferred)   ½ tsp allspice

4c water   ½ tsp cinnamon   1 tsp salt   1/8
tsp cloves   ½ tsp nutmeg

1 apple chopped (optional)

2-3 tbsp peanut oil and/or butter

Combine all ingredients in an ovenproof dish, cover and bake at 425 degrees for about 45 minutes to an hour. Stir and check texture - if it is too watery for you, return to oven uncovered for another 5 minutes.

Baked Steel Cut Oats and Vegetables

Spice pattern: 'The Usual' Indian

This is a middle of January, below-zero windchill type seriously warming dinner. Use McCann's Irish Steel-cut Oats if you can find them.

1 c steel cut oats (McCann's preferred)   2-3 tbsp oil and/or butter

4½ c water   ½ tsp turmeric   1 tsp salt

1 tsp ground coriander   ½ tsp ground cumin

½ tsp allspice   ½ tsp black pepper

1 med onion chopped   1 carrot grated

1 zucchini chopped   1 apple chopped

Combine all ingredients in an ovenproof dish, cover and bake at 425 degrees for about 45 minutes to an hour. Stir and check texture - if it is too watery for you, return to oven uncovered for another 5 minutes.

If desired, serve with Miso-Onion Gravy.

Quinoa Patties

Spice Pattern: Mediterranean

(This recipe is provided by Eve Obert)

Thanks to Deep Gupta for teaching me this recipe. This is really good with a veggie soup, or a cold veggie salad.

| 1 c quinoa | 2 c water | ½ tsp salt |

| ½ tsp basil | ½ tsp oregano | 1 tsp thyme |

3-4 cloves garlic, minced or crushed

1-2 tsp salt or to taste

3 eggs*   (*Note - If you don't want to use eggs, mashed potatoes also works as a binding agent to hold the patties together.)

Optional garnishes

| avocado | sliced tomato |
| feta cheese | salsa |

To cook the quinoa, Wash and rinse well in cold water, rubbing the grain in your hands as you rinse, to remove the bitter outer coating. Strain in a very fine mesh strainer - the grains of quinoa are quite small. Steep as usual, proportion 2 to 1 water to grain, with ½ to 1 tsp salt, for 15 minutes. Set cooked quinoa aside in the fridge for at least a half an hour to cool.

Mix quinoa with the eggs, salt and spices. I suggest just getting in and getting dirty - use your hands. It's actually pretty fun.

Heat oil on medium-low flame, create patties from the mixture, and fry in the oil. Spend enough time on each side, so that each side looks golden brown and crunchy. Serve with optional garnishes or eat plain.

Quinoa Casserole

Spice Pattern: Savory

(This recipe is provided by Eve Obert)

This is a good warming winter dish.

4 cups cooked quinoa. (Roughly 2 cups dry quinoa.)

2 small eggs   1 Tbsp rosemary   1 tsp sage   1 tsp thyme

1 small zucchini   1 yellow bell pepper

1 meduim onion   1 tomato   1 tsp salt

4-5 cloves minced garlic

4 Tbsp olive oil

optional - grated cheese topping

To cook the quinoa, Wash and rinse well in cold water, rubbing the grain in your hands as you rinse, to remove the bitter outer coating. Strain in a very fine mesh strainer - the grains of quinoa are quite small. Steep as usual, proportion 2 to 1 water to grain, with ½ to 1 tsp salt, for 15 minutes.

Saute garlic in olive oil until starting to look a very tiny bit brown. Add chopped onion, Cook until starting to turn "yenem shinley" (a technical Norwegian cooking term meaning translucent and shiny.) Add spices, zucchini and bell pepper. When zucchini and pepper are starting to get soft, add tomato. Cook 5 minutes. Add to cooked quinoa and mix. Put in an oiled casserole dish and cover with lid or aluminum foil. Bake at 350 degrees for 30-45 minutes. Serve and enjoy.

Bean Dishes

Greek Split Pea Soup

Spice pattern: Mediterranean

Olive oil, garlic, lemon, oregano and black pepper give this a Greek flavor. These same seasonings could also be used with lentil soup, or chickpea soup with rice.

3/4 c green or yellow split peas, soaking optional 4 in stick kombu

½ tsp turmeric	1 tsp ginger chopped
½ c white rice	6 c water
½ tbsp olive oil	1 tsp salt or to taste

4 tbsp olive oil	3-4 cloves garlic chopped
1 med onion chopped	
1 tsp oregano	½ tsp black pepper

2-3 tbsp lemon juice *(here the lemon is a foreground taste)*

Boil the split peas with the first group of ingredients, rice, water and a touch of oil for 10 minutes, reduce heat and simmer until the peas are tender (about 45 minutes), then add the salt. Saute the garlic in the olive oil for about 3 min, add the onions and spices and saute on a low flame until the onions are transparent. Add the sauteed vegetable spice mix to the soup, adjust salt and pepper, and cook at least another 10 minutes. Add lemon juice, stir and serve.

Yellow Split Pea Soup

Spice pattern: savory

Start chopping and sauteing the vegetables when the split peas have been cooking about 15 minutes and the vegetables should be ready to add to the soup right about when the split peas are done. You can vary the vegetables and use potatoes, zucchini, eggplant, etc.

3/4 c yellow split peas	6-7 c water
1 tbsp chopped ginger	1 piece kombu or kelp
½ tsp turmeric	1 tsp oil

2 tbsp olive oil

1 jalapeno or serrano chili	1-3 cloves garlic chopped
1 large onion chopped	1 stalk celery chopped
1 red bell pepper chopped	1 large carrot chopped
1 tsp salt 1 tsp basil	1/2 tsp rosemary
1/2 tsp thyme	1/2 tsp black pepper

2 tbsp lemon or lime juice

Bring the split peas to a boil with the kelp, turmeric, ginger and a touch of oil. Keep at a rolling boil uncovered for 10 minutes, then reduce flame to a medium simmer. The peas should be soft and falling apart in about 30-40 minutes.

Saute the serrano (optional) and garlic in the oil until starting to brown. Add the onion, other chopped vegetables, salt and spices, and cook over medium low flame until onions and peppers are soft. Add to the soup when the peas are cooked, adjust salt and add lemon juice, and cook another 10 minutes. Serve.

Red Lentil Soup

Spice pattern: basic

Quick to cook, easy, easy to digest, and very good tasting.

1 c red lentils   5-6 c water

3 inch stick kombu (optional)

2 tbsp olive oil   2-4 tsp ginger chopped (optional)

2 cloves garlic chopped   1 med onion chopped

1 tsp dried dill   1/2 tsp black or white pepper

1 tsp salt or to taste

1 tbsp red wine vinegar or to taste

Cook the lentils and kombu in the water until the red lentils dissolve, about 30 minutes. Start with 5 cups water and add more if you want a thinner soup. Saute the garlic, onion and spices in the oil until onions are transparent. Add to the cooked red lentils and adjust salt. Cook another 5 minutes, add wine vinegar, stir and serve.

You can remove the piece of kombu from the soup, or chop it up and return it to the soup. It should pretty much shred and dissolve in 45 minutes.

Variation: use other vegetables like celery, bell peppers, potatoes, diced tomatoes, eggplant. This is a good, versatile vegetable stew base.

Variation: Try these spice patterns:

   Mediterranean: Omit the dill and use basil.

   Savory: omit dill and use small amounts of basil, rosemary, thyme and sage.

Moong Dal

Spice pattern: 'The Usual' Indian

This soup is one of favorites. It is quick cooking, and gentle, creamy and satisfying tasting. It is is also one of the easiest beans to digest. This recipe can easily be varied by changing spices, or by varying the vegetables.

Bitter melon is a vegetable available in Indian or Oriental groceries.

2/3 c moong dal	6 c water	½ tsp turmeric
1 tsp coriander	2 slices ginger	1 tsp ghee or other oil

1-2 tbsp ghee or other oil	½ tsp cumin seeds
½ tsp salt or to taste	1-2 tbsp lemon juice

One or more of the following vegetables

1 zucchini sliced or chopped	1 med onion chopped
1 c chopped spinach (fresh or frozen)	
1 small bitter melon	1 grated carrot

Cook the moong dal with the water, the first group of spices and a touch of oil until done, about 45 minutes. Add salt to taste, then cook the cumin seeds in the oil until a darker brown. Add vegetables if desired and saute in the oil, then add to soup.

If you are using spinach, do not saute the spinach first - just add it to the soup after the oil and cook 2-3 minutes before adding lemon juice and serving.

If you are using bitter melon, halve the bitter melon and discard the seeds, then simmer the halves in boiling water for 5 minutes. Drain the melon and discard the water. This cuts the strong bitter flavor. Finely chop the melon and add directly to the soup without sauteing.

Simple Blackeyed Peas

Spice pattern: savory

I cook this dish in a slow cooker overnight, but it would work as well cooked stovetop. Spices seem to intensify in a slow cooker so you need smaller amounts of spice for the same effect. It is wonderful with cornbread. The amount of ginger used makes it either a background or foreground taste.

1 c blackeyed peas	3-4 c water
½-2 tsp ginger chopped	½-1 tsp marjoram
1/2 tsp rosemary	black pepper to taste
1-2 pat butter or eqoil	salt to taste (1 tsp or less)

Combine all ingredients except salt and cook the beans until done, overnight in a slow cooker or about 50 minutes to an hour stovetop. Add salt to taste and allow another 10 minutes for the salt to cook in before serving.

Note: If you use ginger paste that has salt, add it after the beans are tender and allow 15-30 minutes for the flavor to merge. Reduce extra salt if necessary.

Variation: add 1 small whole chipotle for a smoky taste,

Variation: For a meat-free version of 'Hoppin John', serve the blackeyes over rice and topped with scallions or with onion relish. Eat on New Year's Day for good fortune for the year.

Lentil Stew

Spice pattern: Savory

2/3 c lentils	1/4 c red lentils (to thicken broth)
6 c water	1 tbsp chopped ginger
½ tsp turmeric	½ tbsp olive oil

1 tsp salt or to taste   black pepper to taste

1 small can diced tomatoes (optional)

3-4 tbsp olive oil   2 cloves garlic chopped

1-2 medium onions chopped

1 tsp basil   1/2 tsp rosemary   1/2 tsp thyme

1/2 tsp sage   1 stalk celery chopped

1 carrot chopped   1 med potato chopped

1-2 tbsp lemon juice or to taste (optional)

Combine both kinds of lentils with water, seasonings and a little bit of oil, bring to a boil and cook about 50 minutes or until all lentils are tender. When the lentils are tender, add the salt and pepper and diced tomatoes. Saute the garlic, onions, celery and spices in the oil until the onions are transparent, add carrots and potatoes, stir and cook another 5 minutes, then add to the stew and stir. Adjust salt and pepper to taste, and cook until potatoes are tender about 10-15 minutes. Add lemon juice a few minutes before serving.

Lentil Tomato Beet Stew

Spice pattern: 'The Usual' Indian

Beets and tomatoes were made for each other.

2/3 c lentils   1/4 c red lentils   6 c water

1 tbsp chopped ginger   ½ tsp turmeric

½ tsp whole fennel seeds   1 tsp ground coriander

½ tsp cumin   ½ tbsp peanut or olive oil

3-4 medium beets, chopped

1/2 tsp salt or to taste black pepper to taste

1 small can diced tomatoes

3-4 tbsp peanut or olive oil   2 cloves garlic chopped

1-2 medium onions chopped

1-2 tbsp lemon juice or to taste (optional)

Combine both kinds of lentils and chopped beets with water, seasonings and a little bit of oil, bring to a boil and cook about 50 minutes or until all lentils are tender. When the lentils are tender, add the salt and pepper and diced tomatoes. Saute the garlic and onions in the oil until the onions are transparent, add to the stew and stir. Adjust salt and pepper to taste, and cook at least another 10 minutes. Add lemon juice if desired, but go light with it - in this dish it is a background taste. Serve.

Mexican Black Bean Soup

Spice pattern: Mexican

Black beans and epazote are a marriage made in heaven. Dried epazote is available in Mexican markets as is the chipotle, or you can find them by mail order fairly easily. Use the chipotle if you like a smoky and slightly hot flavor. I think this one gets better with reheating for a couple of days.

1 c black beans, soaked and drained	1 tsp dried epazote
6 c water	½ tsp salt or to taste
1-2 slices ginger	½ tsp olive oil

3-4 tbsp olive oil	½ tsp turmeric	3-4 cloves garlic chopped
1 small chipotle chili (optional)		1 medium onion chopped
1 stalk celery chopped		1 tbsp lemon juice or to taste

Slow Cooker: Boil the soaked black beans in 6 cups water for about 10 minutes, then add them with the first group of spices, chipotle and a touch of oil to a slow cooker and cook overnight or until beans are tender. Add the epazote and salt when you start sauteing the vegetables.

Stovetop: Boil the beans as above, and add the first group of spices and the epazote and cook until tender, about 1-1/2 to 2 hours. Add salt.

Saute the garlic, onion and celery in the oil until the onions are transparent, and add them to the soup. Adjust salt and cook at least another 30 minutes slow cooker or 10 minutes stovetop to let the flavors blend. Add lemon juice, stir and serve.

Variation: When the beans are cooked, chop the chipotle and add it back to the soup for a hotter taste. Leave the chipotle whole or remove it if you like a milder taste.

Slow Cooker Variation: Add the sauteed vegetables and epazote to the slow cooker at the same time you add the beans before the slow cooking time. The only ingredients you hold until the beans are tender are the salt and lemon juice. This adds a little bit of cooking effort up front and reduces the cooking effort at the end.

Black Beans with Potatoes and Chilis

Spice pattern: Mexican

Potato soaks up hot spices, so this dish is not that hot at all. To make the dish very mild either discard the jalapeno seeds, or use a green bell pepper or an anaheim pepper. There is enough cilantro in this dish that it acts more like a green vegetable than a garnish.

Substitute parsley if you don't like cilantro - flat parsley works better, I think.

This dish is a good simple meal with whole wheat toast, or stuffed into a pita bread. Yogurt on the side makes a nice complement if you do dairy, but it isn't necessary.

3-4 tbsp olive oil   4 medium potatoes, chopped into small cubes

2 c cooked black beans   (or, 1 can black beans)

1 tsp whole cumin seeds   2-3 cloves garlic

1-2 jalapenos, finely chopped   ½ c cilantro, chopped

1-2 tbsp lemon or lime juice, or to taste   salt to taste

Saute the cumin seeds in the oil until they change color. Add the garlic and peppers, saute about 3 minutes more, then add the onions and saute another 3-4 min. Add the chopped potatoes, turn the flame very low and cook until potatoes are tender, about 10-15 min. Add water if needed to keep the potatoes from burning Add the black beans and heat through. Add the lemon or lime juice and cilantro, stir and serve.

Black Bean Chili

Spice pattern: Mexican

Ground dried chilis, with cumin, oregano, garlic and onion, together make up the spice mix we know as chili powder. In this recipe you making your own chili mix of spices, so you have more control over the taste. None of the chilis I use here are particularly hot, so this probably comes out as a mild to medium chili. I use the dried chilis cut up into small pieces in this recipe, but they could also be ground together with the cumin and oregano to make your own chili powder.

Chili is best tasting made a day in advance.

1½ c black beans	6 c water
½ tsp turmeric	2 tsp oil

4 tbsp olive oil	1 tsp whole cumin seeds
2 ancho chilis, cut up	2 guajillo chilis, cut up
4 cloves garlic chopped	2 med onion chopped
2 green bell peppers chopped	1 tsp salt or to taste
1 tsp oregano	1 small can tomato paste
1 large can diced tomatoes	½ c hearty red wine (like burgundy)

Boil the black beans with the water, kombu, turmeric and a touch of oil for 10 minutes, then reduce heat and gently boil until done, about 90 minutes. Or, cook in a slow cooker for about 6-8 hours or overnight after boiling for 10 minutes.

Heat the oil and cook the cumin seeds and dried chili pieces until the cumin seeds turn a darker brown. Add garlic and cook another 2-3 minutes. Add the onions, bell peppers and spices and cook until onions are soft and transparent. Add the tomato paste and stir, and fry the tomato paste over a low flame until it darkens and becomes crumbly textured and glistens with the oil. Add the cooked beans with maybe a cup of their cooking liquid, the diced tomatoes and wine. Adjust spices if you need to, bring to a simmer and just let it cook, at least another hour, the longer the better.

Chickpea Red Lentil Stew

Spice pattern: 'The usual' Indian

This recipe is an example of using red lentils with another bean to thicken the soup. Moong dal can be used similarly.

You can substitute zucchini for chayote.

1-2 c cooked chickpeas	2-3 tbsp peanut oil
1 tsp chopped ginger	
7 c water total (incl. cooking liquid)	1 med onion chopped
2/3 c red lentils	1 tsp coriander	½ tsp cumin
½ tsp turmeric	½ tsp black pepper

2 chayote chopped	1 carrot chopped
1 parsnip chopped	½ tsp salt
1 tbsp lemon juice	cilantro or flat parsley garnish (optional)

Cook the red lentils with the chickpeas, water and cooking liquid, plus the kombu, turmeric, and chayote if you are using it. The red lentils should dissolve in less than 30 minutes. Saute the ginger and onion with the spices until onions are transparent. Add carrots, parsnips (and zucchini if you are using it), stir and saute another 3-5 minutes, then add the sauteed veggies to the soup, adjust salt, and cook another 10 to 15 minutes to let the flavors blend. Add lemon juice and garnish, stir and serve.

Mediterranean Beans and Vegetables

Spice pattern: Mediterranean

This recipe will work with pretty much any cooked whole bean, including black beans, small red beans and navy beans, and each type of bean will change the taste of the dish.

2-4 tbsp olive oil	½-1 tsp ginger chopped
2-3 cloves garlic chopped	1 medium onion chopped

1 green or red bell pepper, chopped

salt and black pepper to taste

1 tsp basil	1 tsp oregano	½ tsp marjoram (optional)

2 c cooked beans (favas, garbanzos, pintos)

or 1 can cooked beans

1 tbsp lemon juice or to taste	parsley or cilantro to garnish

Saute the ginger and garlic in the olive oil for 2-3 minutes, then add the onions, bell peppers and spices and saute until vegetables are at desired level of doneness. Add the cooked beans and heat through thoroughly, then cook another few minutes for the tastes to merge. Add lemon juice and garnish, stir and serve.

Variation: For Mediterranean beans and rice, stir in 3-4 cups cooked rice.

Variation: This would go really well with a small can of tomato sauce added.

Dips and Relishes

Lentil Dip with Onion Relish

Spice pattern: basic

This mild and smooth dip is good by itself, and wonderful with Onion Relish.

1 c lentils	2 slices ginger
1/2 tsp turmeric	1/2 tsp fennel seeds
1 tsp olive oil	3-1/2 c water
1 tsp salt or to taste	½ tsp black pepper to taste

3 tbsp olive oil	1 pat butter (optional but nice)
1 med onion finely chopped	1 stalk celery finely chopped
2 tbsp lemon juice	

Cook the lentils with the first group of ingredients, water and a bit of oil, until tender, about 50 minutes. Check during cooking to see if you need more water. When tender, add salt and pepper to taste and let sit 5 minutes, drain lentils and reserve the cooking liquid, then puree the lentils while still warm - the mix will thicken as it cools. (I like to use an immersion blender.)

Use just enough of the cooking liquid to smoothly puree the lentils. Meanwhile slowly saute the onion and celery over a low flame in the oil and butter until the onions are very soft, about 10 to 15 minutes. Combine the sauteed vegetables with the puree, add lemon juice and adjust salt and pepper. Allow to cool before serving.

Hummus Tahini (Chickpea Dip)

Spice pattern: basic

This is a very popular Middle Eastern dip. It goes well with pita bread and tabouli salad as a good light meal when the weather is warm, or as a side dish with pita and a hot rice or bulghur main course when the weather is cold.

Adjust the garlic, olive oil, lemon juice, tahini and salt until you get the level of smoothness or sharpness you want. Note that you need fresh garlic cloves for this to taste right.

If you leave out the tahini, try increasing the olive oil a little; you will still have a good dip that isn't quite as smooth or rich.

1 c chickpeas, soaked	4 in stick kombu
½ tsp turmeric 1 tsp olive oil	4 c water

¼ - ½ c olive oil	3-10 cloves garlic, pressed or chopped
3-6 tbsp lemon juice	1-2 tsp salt or to taste
2-4 tbsp tahini	

Boil the drained beans for about 10 minutes, then cook the beans with the first group of ingredients until tender (25 min in a pressure cooker, overnight in a slow cooker.) When tender, add salt to the cooking water, stir and let sit 5 minutes.

Puree the chickpeas while still warm with all other ingredients except the tahini, using just enough of the cooking liquid to get a smooth puree. Adjust the ingredients to taste, and stir in a bowl with the tahini when you have the garlic amount you want pureed in. Refrigerate at least an hour for the flavors to combine before serving.

Chickpea Dip

Spice pattern: Basic

This is a simple sandwich spread or dip in which the scallions are the predominant taste. It is similar to hummus.

1 c chickpeas or other bean

1 slice ginger

4 in stick kombu   1 tsp olive oil

4 c water

1 tsp salt or to taste

4 tbsp olive oil   ½ tsp black pepper

4-6 scallions finely chopped, or 1/4 c sweet onion

4 cloves garlic, pressed or finely chopped

2-3 tbsp lemon juice

Boil the drained beans for about 10 minutes, then cook the beans with the first group of ingredients, preferably in a pressure cooker, until tender (90 min in a pressure cooker, about 3 hours stovetop.) When tender, add salt to the cooking water, stir and let sit 5 minutes. Puree the beans while still warm, using just enough of the cooking liquid to get a smooth puree - you can throw the kombu in with the puree if you want. Combine with the rest of the ingredients and stir well. Refrigerate at least an hour for the flavors to combine before serving.

Variation: Add mayonnaise, and/or chopped olives with pimentos. Add chili sauce, flakes or powder if you like heat.

Tofu-Dill Dip with Variations

Spice pattern: basic

Quick and easy to make, smooth and creamy. This also works as a salad dressing. Silken tofu has the best texture for this.

Sometimes some of the liquid in the dip will settle out in the refrigerator after a day or two. Just stir before serving.

3 tbsp olive oil

1 clove garlic

2 tbsp red wine vinegar or lemon juice

2 scallions, roughly chopped

½-1 tsp salt

1/2 tsp black pepper

2 tsp dried dill

1 cake (10 oz) firm or extra firm tofu, drained

just enough water to puree (or, if you mash with a fork instead of using a blender, omit the water. That will give you a rougher texture dip.)

Combine ingredients in a blender in the order listed, and puree until smooth. Adjust seasoning and stir some more until you get the mix you want. Serve.

Variations:

Tofu-scallion dip - omit the dill and use 4-6 scallions.

Tofu-spinach dip - combine the pureed tofu-dill dip with a thawed package of chopped spinach and stir - do not puree the spinach. Increase pepper and garlic if desired.

For a lighter taste, substitute lemon or lime juice for the red wine vinegar. For a sharper taste, use plain white vinegar. You may need to adjust amounts.

Balsamic vinegar tastes good in this dip, but it turns the color muddy brown. (This works as a tofu-balsamic mayonnaise substitute for potato or pasta salads.)

Creamy tofu pasta sauce - heat the dip until very warm but not boiling before stirring into the hot pasta, and garnish with fresh scallions or parsley. You may want to make the dip stronger tasting, more salty and sour, to use it this way.

As always, add hot chili to taste.

Aduki Bean Ginger Dip

Like the hummus dip, this dip can very from gentle to sharp depending on how much ginger and cayenne you use.

The lemon juice has a lighter taste, and the red wine vinegar gives a sharper bite, so you can vary the proportions to suit your preference.

1 cup aduki beans, soaked   2-3 tbsp peanut oil or other oil

3-4 c water   1 tsp salt or to taste   1 piece kombu

2 tsp lemon juice   2 tsp red wine vinegar

3-6 tbsp roughly chopped ginger

1 tsp oil   ¼ - 1 tsp cayenne or other hot chili

Cook the aduki beans in water with kombu, turmeric and a touch of oil until tender, about 45 minutes stovetop or 15 minutes pressure cooker. Drain and reserve the liquid.

Puree the adukis with the remaining ingredients until smooth. It works best to puree them while still warm since they thicken when they cool. Add some of the cooking liquid if you need it to get a smooth creamy paste. Adjust seasonings to get the level of sharpness and sourness you want. Chill before serving.

Steamed Eggplant Dip

Spice pattern: basic

Most recipes I have seen for eggplant dip call for roasting the eggplant first. I use steaming because it is quicker and easier and still makes a good tasting dip.

2-3 large eggplant, cut in ¾ inch slices

½-1 tsp salt   3-4 tbsp olive oil

2-4 cloves garlic, pressed or finely chopped

2-4 tbsp lemon juice   ¼-½ tsp cayenne pepper

Steam the eggplant until soft, in the range of 5-10 minutes. Scoop out the pulpy center into a bowl and discard the skins. Combine with the other ingredients and adjust flavors. Allow to cool at least an hour before serving.

Variations:

Add a half a chopped red onion and a diced tomato.

This is another dip that works with mayonnaise if you like it richer.

Onion Relish

I usually make this with red onions, but it works with most other kinds as well. Sweet onions would be particularly good. It is wonderful with lentil dip or other bean dip on crackers, or as a garnish for chili, or over a rice or bean dish where a little extra sharp bite would enhance the taste. My daughter likes it with yogurt over rice. Or maybe over a salad or with a sandwich spread. Or...

I suggest serving this in a side bowl so that your diners can add it as they choose. It's nice to have the relish on only a bite here and there, as a change of pace.

This is at its best the first 3 days after you make it, then it gradually loses its bite without spoiling.

I've eaten and enjoyed it over a week after making it.

1-2 medium onions, finely chopped   (about ¾ cup chopped)

½-1 tsp salt or to taste

1 tbsp lemon juice or to taste

1/8-1/4 tsp cayenne (optional)

Combine ingredients, stir and refrigerate at least an hour before serving.

Variations:

As usual, you can substitute vinegar for a sharper taste.

As usual, add hot chili spice to taste.

(Do you see the pattern to the variations? Do you see why I say that most cookbooks only have a handful of recipes plus variations? You have all the flavor tools now. Play with them.)

Salads

Rice and Vegetable Salad Sample

This is just an example of a rice and vegetable salad. The All Purpose Rice and Vegetable Salad Pattern earlier in the book describes how to vary it.

2 c short grain brown rice

4 c water

½ tsp salt

6-8 scallions chopped

1 package frozen peas

1 package frozen corn

2-4 tbsp red wine vinegar

3-4 tbsp olive or peanut oil

1 tbsp dried dill

½ tsp salt or to taste

1 red bell pepper chopped

½ tsp black pepper

Pressure cook the brown rice for 50 minutes, or stovetop cook for 50 minutes to an hour, until all water is absorbed and rice is soft and mildly sweet. Always let rice sit 5-10 minutes after cooking before opening pot.

Put the frozen vegetables in a salad bowl, then add the hot cooked rice and stir. The hot rice will thaw the vegetables, and the frozen vegetables will cool the rice.

Add other ingredients, stir and adjust seasonings.

Caribbean Salad with Chickpeas

Spice pattern: basic

This is my version of a salad that a Caribbean restaurant in Minneapolis serves. The interesting mix of vegetables with chickpeas needs only a very simple seasoning.

1½ c green cabbage, chopped or grated

1½ c red cabbage, chopped or grated

1-2 carrots, grated

1 cucumber, quartered and sliced

2-3 roma or regular tomatoes, chopped

(or equivalent cherry tomatoes)

1½ c cooked chickpeas

or 1 can chickpeas, drained

2 tbsp olive oil

salt and black pepper to taste

1-2 tbsp lemon juice

Combine all ingredients, except the lemon juice and toss. Add the lemon juice, toss again, adjust seasoning and serve.

Tabouli Salad

Spice pattern: Mediterranean

"Authentic" tabouli salad, a very popular Middle Eastern dish, has parsley as the main ingredient. This tabouli recipe is lighter on the parsley and heavier on the grain so it can serve as a main course dish.

1 c bulghur (cracked wheat)

1/2 tsp salt 2 c water

2-4 tbsp or more olive oil

1 tbsp dried mint

2-4 cloves garlic, pressed or chopped

6-8 scallions, chopped

½ - 1 cup finely chopped parsley

1 green bell pepper, chopped (optional)

1 large cucumber, quartered and sliced

½-1 pint cherry tomatoes, halved

salt and black pepper to taste

3-4 tbsp lemon juice

Cook the bulghur with the water and salt for 15 minutes. Allow the bulghur to cool. While the bulghur is cooling, add the other ingredients to a salad bowl in the order listed, stirring after each one is added. (The spice ingredients are added first to permeate the oil.) Add the bulghur and stir, then add the lemon juice. Adjust seasonings, including amount of olive oil, to taste, and serve.

Variation: substituting cilantro for parsley also makes an excellent salad, although strictly speaking it is then no longer tabouli.

Varying proportions, this can be primarily a vegetable salad, or primarily a bulghur salad.

Chickpea Rice Salad

Spice pattern: Savory

This is a very pretty salad visually, with the bright red bell peppers and tomatoes, the bright yellow chickpeas, the bright green scallions and parsley, and the white rice. The proportion of beans to grain in this salad is about 1:1. so I like to have some crackers on the side. I used short grain white rice, but another rice could be used also.

1 c chickpeas, soaked

1 piece kombu	1/2 tsp turmeric	
2 slices ginger	1 tsp oil	4 c water

½ tsp salt or to taste	4 tbsp peanut or olive oil
2-3 cloves garlic	1 tsp marjoram
½ tsp sage 1 tsp rosemary	1/2 tsp thyme
1/2 tsp black pepper or to taste	6-8 scallions chopped
½-1 pint cherry tomatoes, halved	1 red bell pepper chopped
1/2 c parsley chopped	2 c cooked rice

Boil the drained beans for about 10 minutes, then cook the beans with the first group of ingredients, preferably in a pressure cooker, until tender (25 min in a pressure cooker.) When tender, add salt to the cooking water, stir and let sit 5 minutes. Add the other ingredients to a salad bowl in the order listed, stirring after each one is added. (The spice ingredients are added first to permeate the oil.) Add the chickpeas and rice and stir, then add the vinegar. Adjust seasonings to taste and serve.

Potato Salad with Chickpeas

Spice pattern: 'The Usual' Indian

6 large potatoes   3 tbsp olive oil

1 red bell pepper, chopped

1/2 c parsley (Italian preferred), chopped

1½ c cooked chickpeas or 1 can chickpeas, drained and rinsed

1 tsp grated or finely chopped ginger

1 tsp ground coriander (freshly ground is nice)

¼ tsp turmeric   1/2 tsp black pepper

1/2 tsp salt or to taste

2-3 tbsp balsamic vinegar

Boil the potatoes in lightly salted water in their skins until soft (about 15-20 minutes), drain and allow to cool. Peel if desired, and chop in large chunks.

Combine all ingredients in a salad bowl except the vinegar and stir - the potatoes should turn yellow from the turmeric. Adjust salt and pepper and add the balsamic and stir. Refrigerate before serving, preferably for at least an hour for the spices to blend.

Variations: I hope you see that you have an approximately infinite number of variations on bean-potato salad by varying the bean, the seasoning pattern, the vinegar or sauce, other vegetables, and so on.

Even making a dish like this with a bean of a distinctly different color can make a difference in the dish.

Pressed Cabbage Salad

Spice pattern: basic

This is a very plain light salad that goes well as a side course to a substantial main dish. The cabbage is very lightly pickled from the salt and pressure, which softens it. The wakame doesn't affect the taste and adds nutrition. (See the section on Seaweed in part one).

4 c cabbage (green, red or both), finely chopped

2 tsp salt

4 scallions, chopped   1 carrot, grated

½ tsp black pepper

wakame, soaked and chopped (optional) (about 1/8 c total)

1-2 tbsp lemon juice

Mix the cabbage and salt in a bowl, then place a plate that fits in the bowl over the cabbage, and place a weight on the plate - I use a half gallon closed jar filled with water. Let the cabbage sit under the weight at room temperature for 4-8 hours. Drain the cabbage and squeeze it to ring out some of the excess moisture and salt, combine with the remaining ingredients and toss. Chill and serve.

Variation: When I don't want to wait for the cabbage to press and be very wilted, I will just stir and squeeze the cabbage with my hands for a couple of minutes. It will become wet quite quickly, and a just a bit less crunchy. I always include this step any time I make a salad with cabbage.

Spicy Cabbage Salad

Spice pattern: basic

2-3 tbsp olive oil

2 cloves garlic, pressed or chopped

1 tsp oregano

1/2 tsp black pepper   ¼ tsp or more cayenne or hot chili

1/2 c grated daikon radish   or chopped red radish

1-2 carrots grated

wakame, soaked and chopped (optional)   (about 1/8 c total)

4 c cabbage (green, red or both), finely chopped

½ tsp salt or to taste

2-3 tbsp red wine vinegar

Combine ingredients and mix - I like to add them to the salad bowl in the order listed, mixing after each so that the spices blend. Chill before serving.

Variation: use pressed cabbage, or quick-pressed cabbage, instead of raw cabbage, and omit or reduce any added salt.

Creamy Coleslaw

This is completely dairy-free, but it has the richness of a good creamy coleslaw.

4 c cabbage (red, green or both) chopped

1 carrot grated   1/2 c white or red radish, grated

6-8 scallions chopped   2 cloves garlic chopped

1/2 tsp black pepper or to taste   2-3 tbsp olive oil

 1/2 tsp salt or to taste

2-3 tbsp sesame tahini

1/4 c water (as needed to thin dressing)

2-3 tbsp red wine vinegar

Combine all ingredients up through the olive oil and salt and toss to coat vegetables. Stir in the sesame tahini with just enough water to give you the texture of dressing you want. Stir in the vinegar and adjust seasonings. This can be served immediately, but I think it gets better after standing for 30 minutes to let the flavors blend.

Take into account, when you make this, that the dressing will likely get thicker and drier as it sits refrigerated.

Cooked Vegetables

Potatoes with Brown Mustard Seeds

Spice pattern: 'The usual' Indian

3 tbsp peanut or other oil   or peanut oil with a pat of butter

(you also use just ghee for a very rich taste)

1 tsp brown mustard seeds

1 green bell pepper, chopped

¼ tsp turmeric   1/2 tsp ground coriander

1/2 tsp salt   1/2 tsp black pepper

3 large potatoes, cut in ½ in chunks   ¼ c water

1 tsp lemon juice

Heat the oil and cook the mustard seeds covered until they begin to pop. Add the bell pepper and saute about 3-5 minutes. Add the rest of the spices, the potatoes and the water, cover, reduce to a low flame and cook until potatoes are tender, about 15- 20 minutes. Check periodically to see if you need more water to keep the mix from burning.

When the potatoes are done, uncover and cook another few minutes if the dish is wetter than you want. Add lemon juice, heat another 2-3 minutes, and serve.

Variations:

• Omit the mustard seeds and use whole cumin seeds instead. Cook the cumin seeds in the oil until they turn a darker brown, then proceed with recipe.

• For a spicier dish, add some seeded and chopped small green chilis to the oil after the seeds, and cook them for 2-3 minutes before adding the bell pepper.

Cooked Spicy Cabbage

Spice pattern: 'The usual' Indian

2-3 tbsp peanut or other oil

1 tsp whole brown mustard seeds   1 tsp whole cumin seeds

1-2 small green chilis, seeded and chopped

1-2 med onions chopped

3 c cabbage (green, red or both), finely chopped

1/2 tsp salt or to taste ¼ tsp black pepper 2 tbsp lemon juice

Heat the oil, add the brown mustard and cumin seeds, and cook until the mustard seeds pop - cover the pan since they can spatter. Quickly add the green chilis and cover again, and cook for another minute. Add the onions and saute until they are transparent. Add cabbage and the remaining seasoning and cook until the cabbage is tender - you may want to add ¼ cup of water to very lightly steam the cabbage. Add the lemon juice and adjust seasonings about 5 minutes before serving. Serve hot.

Variation: Omit chilis and use 2-4 tsp of chopped fresh ginger to add pungency.

Collard Greens and Potatoes for One

This is an easy way to cook a single portion of collards and potatoes. It is nice being able to cook the greens without having to make a big batch all at once and then have leftovers. Obviously you can adjust amounts if you are cooking for multiple people.

1-2 large Collard leaves, chopped

1 small to medium potato, chopped in medium cubes

garlic

olive oil, butter or or ghee

fish sauce or salt to taste

vinegar

hot sauce

1 cup water

Saute the collards and garlic in the oil while you heat the water. When the water is boiling, pour it over the collards - I add water to about 1/3 inch depth. Add fish sauce or salt, vinegar and hot sauce. Place the potatoes in the pot on top of the collards and cover. Cook for around 20 minutes or until the potatoes are thoroughly done. I like to mash in some of the potatoes, and leave some chunks.

Check part way through to make sure you still have enough cooking water. I like to have just a little bit of liquid left as a sauce when it's done, but not enough to be a soup.

Tofu and Spinach

Spice pattern: 'The Usual' Indian

The turmeric turns the tofu a bright yellow, so this dish looks like scrambled eggs and spinach. It is a quick and easy light meal with whole wheat toast.

2-4 tbsp peanut or other oil   or oil & butter, or ghee

1 small green chili, seeded and chopped

1 med onion chopped   1/2 tsp turmeric

1/2 tsp coriander   1/2 tsp cumin

1/2 tsp salt or to taste

1 package (about 10 oz) firm or extra firm tofu, drained and cut in ½ in cubes

1 package (about 12 oz) frozen chopped spinach

or equivalent fresh spinach, chopped

1 tbsp lemon juice

Heat the oil, cook the chilis in the oil about 3 minutes, then add the onion and spices and cook on a low flame until the onions are soft, the longer the better. Add the tofu, stir and cook uncovered while the tofu absorbs the spices. Add spinach, stir and heat through. Adjust salt, add lemon juice and serve.

Sauteed Squash with Onions and Spices

Spice pattern: warming

This is a quick and delicious side dish that is a good way to use leftover baked winter squash.

3-4 tbsp olive oil, ghee or butter

1 med onion chopped

1/8 tsp cardamom

¼ tsp nutmeg

½ tsp salt or to taste

1-2 tsp ginger finely chopped

¼ tsp allspice

1/8 tsp cloves

1/8 tsp black pepper

2 c cooked winter squash (butternut or acorn), mashed

Heat the oil, add the ginger and onions and spices, cook until the onions are translucent. Add the mashed cooked squash and heat through, stirring occasionally. Serve.

Variation: Add chopped pistachios. Or for a sweeter dish, add ¼ c raisins soaked in a cup in enough hot water to cover.

Slow Cooker Root Vegetables

Spice pattern: none

This is a really convenient way to cook a couple of beets, yams or potatoes without turning on the oven.

Root vegetable - beet, sweet potato or yam, potato, turnip

Wash the vegetable and leave it a bit damp. Loosely wrap in tinfoil and place in the slow cooker. Cook on high for roughly 2-3 hours until done. Cooking time will vary according to the size of the vegetable - I use a smell test to tell when it's done.

Option: Potatoes or yams are good if you very lightly oil the skin before wrapping it in tinfoil and cooking.

Oven Roasted Vegetables

Spice pattern: plain, Mediterranean or savory

This is a tasty and warming side dish. It is good plain, and very good with tofu-dill dip or tofu-scallion dip. It makes a good light meal with whole wheat toast and a cup of pea soup, and it makes a good breakfast with toast and tofu 'scrambled eggs'.

3 medium potatoes	1-2 large carrots
1 medium onion	1/2 tsp salt
1/2 tsp pepper	1/2 tsp basil
1/2 tsp rosemary or 1/2 tsp oregano	
2-3 tbsp olive oil or ghee or butter	

Preheat oven to 350 degrees. Roughly chop the vegetables onto a cookie sheet, add the spices and oil and stir thoroughly with your hands to coat the vegetable with the oil and spices. Cook in the oven for about 20-35 minutes, until the potatoes are cooked through and the vegetables have a golden brown underside. Be careful not to let the undersides get too dark or the vegetables will taste burnt. Serve hot, either plain or with a tofu-dill or tofu-scallion dip.

This also works well cooked in a toaster oven.

Soups (not Bean Based)

Miso Vegetable Soup

Spice pattern: Oriental (the miso is the spice pattern)

This is a good simple, warming and easy to digest soup that can be made from scratch in about a half an hour. The miso tastes best if you add just enough to make the soup rich tasting without getting very salty.

1-2 tbsp peanut, sesame or other oil

1 med onion finely chopped   1 stalk celery finely chopped

1 carrot grated

wakame, soaked and chopped (optional)   (about 1/8 c total)

1/4 tsp black pepper (optional)   4 c water

miso - about 1-2 tsp per serving bowl

chopped scallions for garnish

Saute the onions, celery and carrots in the oil over a low flame for 5-10 minutes or until they are soft. Add the water and wakame, bring to a boil, cover and simmer about 15 minutes.

For best taste, the miso is added at the time of serving in each individual bowl. To do this, take 1-2 tsp of miso in a bowl, add a little bit of the broth and stir the miso to thin it to sauce texture. Add the serving amount to the bowl, stir and check the seasoning. If you need more miso it can be added in small amounts and mashed on the side of the bowl. Garnish with a sprinkling of chopped scallions and serve.

Variation: This soup is also nice with small cubes of firm tofu added to the broth.

Artsy Butternut Squash Almond Butter Soup

Spice pattern: neo-trendy ('The Usual' Indian mostly)

Very delicious, and to be used to impress your friends with how very hip your vegetarian cooking skills are. (Actually, I thought of this soup as an example of a recipe that sounds more exotic and trendy than 'split pea soup'.)

The recipe is a good example of how nut butters can be used to add a creamy thickness to soups. They work well with sweet vegetables like winter squash, or carrot and parsnip. Peanut and cashew butter also work well used this way.

1 large butternut squash   2-4 tbsp almond butter

peanut oil   or other nut butter

½-1 tsp salt or to taste

2 tbsp peanut oil   ½ tsp black pepper or to taste

1 tsp brown mustard seeds

1 tsp finely chopped ginger   fresh chopped cilantro garnish

½ tsp turmeric   1 tsp coriander

1 med onion chopped   ½ tsp cumin

grated kefalotyri cheese garnish

(or other imported, hard to pronounce sharp grating cheese)

4 c water

Cut the butternut squash in half, scoop out and remove seeds. Coat cut sides with peanut oil, and bake in a 375 degree oven until tender, about 45 minutes. Allow to cool enough to handle.

In your soup pan, heat the oil and add the brown mustard seeds, cover and cook the seeds until they start to pop and spatter. Reduce heat to low, add the ginger, onion and spices and cook onions slowly until very soft, at least 15 minutes, the longer the better. It's okay if the onions start to brown. Add the water. Scoop the cooked squash out of its skin, mash and add to the water - a wire whisk will smooth the texture of the soup. Cook another 5 minutes, then add the almond butter, salt and pepper and stir to get a very smooth soup. Adjust salt and pepper if necessary, and cook another 5 minutes on low heat.

Serve in bowls sprinkled with finely chopped cilantro and the grated-hard-to pronounce cheese. (Romano or parmesan will do in a pinch, but make sure they are imported and expensive. It works best with cheeses that have at least four syllable names.)

Creamy Parsnip Oat Soup

Spice pattern: basic, savory

The rolled oats and tahini together make this soup creamy and rich, and they complement the sweetness of the parsnips. The miso is salty, but if you use just the right amount it further enhances the sweetness of the other ingredients without making the soup taste salty. Start with the smaller amount of miso, and only add more if the soup tastes flat.

2 tbsp peanut or other oil	½ tsp chopped ginger
1 med onion, finely chopped	1/2 tsp marjoram ¼ tsp salt
1/2 tsp black pepper	4-5 parsnips, finely chopped
4 c water	1/3 c rolled oats
2 tbsp tahini (adjust to taste)	1-2 tbsp miso
parsley garnish (optional)	

Saute the ginger, onion and spices in the oil over a low flame until the onion turns transparent, about 5 minutes. Add the parsnips, stir and saute another 3 minutes. Add water and rolled oats, bring to a boil, reduce heat to low and simmer about 15 minutes - the parsnips should be very tender and the oats should be pretty much dissolved in the water. Add the tahini, stir and cook on very low flame another 3 minutes or so. Mash the miso with 5-6 tbsp of the broth to thin it out, and stir it into the soup. Taste and adjust miso if needed/ Simmer another 2-3 minutes, then serve.

Variation: Small amounts of other savory spices (thyme, nutmeg, rosemary) could be used to good effect.

Vegetable Tomato Barley Soup

spice pattern: savory

There are no peas or beans in this soup, so all of the flavor comes from the slowly sauteed vegetables and spices in the oil. So, take your time on the saute step and let the onions soften slowly.

3 tbsp peanut or other oil	1 stalk celery chopped
1 tsp ginger chopped	1 large carrot chopped
2 cloves garlic chopped	2 med potatoes chopped
1 large onion chopped	4 c water
½ tsp salt or to taste	½ c pearl barley
1 tsp basil	1 piece kombu
½ tsp rosemary	1 lg can diced tomatoes
½ tsp black pepper	½ tsp thyme
1 tsp lemon juice	

Heat the oil ad cook the ginger and garlic 2-3 minutes. Add the onions, celery and spices and cook until onions are very soft, about 10 minutes. Add carrots and potatoes, stir and cook another 5 minutes. Add remaining ingredients, bring to a boil, reduce heat and simmer for about an hour or until barley is thoroughly cooked.

Sauces

Serious Tomato Sauce

Spice pattern: Mediterranean

This is a 'genuine' Italian tomato sauce recipe. I learned it from 'genuine' Italian relatives while growing up in New York City.

The 'secret' to a thick and crumbly textured tomato sauce is to fry the tomato paste with the garlic and oil until it crumbles and darkens, almost until it burns. For a cooking wine I use a hearty inexpensive red wine like burgundy. The tomato puree makes a very thick and heavy sauce, the diced tomatoes a little less so.

To do this one right, the sauce really needs to cook all day or overnight. Once the frying step is finished, the rest of the ingredients can be combined in a slow cooker. It gets better with time.

4 tbsp olive oil (or more)   1-2 whole dried red chilis

or 1-2 tsp dried guajillo chili pieces

3-4 cloves garlic, chopped

1 small (6 oz) can tomato paste

1 lg can (28 oz) tomato puree or diced tomatoes

½ c (or more) hearty burgundy or similar red wine

or 1 tbsp brown sugar (if you can't deal with the wine)

1 tsp basil   1 tsp oregano

½ tsp mint (optional)   1-2 bay leaves

1 stick kombu or kelp (optional)

1/2 tsp salt or to taste

½ tsp black pepper

Heat the oil over a low flame, and fry the red chilis and garlic until the garlic just starts to brown. Add the tomato paste, stir and fry, stirring occasionally, until the paste is crumbly and browning and appears coated with the oil. Don't rush this step - you can fry the paste to where it starts to burn a little bit. When you stir you may need to scrape the paste off the bottom of the pan where it sticks. Add the rest of the ingredients, stir, put on a very low flame or slow cooker, and just let it cook covered, stirring occasionally (less often with a slow cooker) for as long as you can, 4-6 hours minimum. The sauce tastes as good or better reheated the second day.

Variation: Add extra vegetables - onions, bell peppers or anaheim peppers, mushrooms - by sauteing them on the side in a little bit of olive oil and mixing them in with the sauce after the paste is finished frying.

Spaghetti and Mock Duck with Tomato Sauce

This is a serving suggestion for pasta with sauce. The mock duck fried with the onions has a chewy, meaty texture and works with the spaghetti and sauce. If you like a pasta, butter and onion kind of taste, the mock duck and spaghetti stirred together without the tomato sauce works well also.

Cooked spaghetti

Serious Tomato Sauce (see previous recipe)

or other tomato sauce

(use a store bought sauce if you want - I won't tell)

2-3 tbsp olive oil   2 medium onions, chopped

1 sm can wheat gluten (mock duck)

salt and pepper to taste

Fry the onions in the olive oil until translucent, then add the mock duck, season to taste and saute for a couple of minutes. Cook the spaghetti according to package directions, and toss with a little bit of olive oil or butter while still very hot. Serve the spaghetti topped with the mock duck and onions with the tomato sauce added. Or, have the pasta with sauce with the mock duck on the side.

Variation: This would work well with a hearty bean like red kidney beans instead of the mock duck. You would then have a variant on a classic Italian dish, Pasta E Fagioli, pasta and beans. Of course, beans don't have the chewy mock duck texture.

Onion Miso Gravy

Spice pattern: basic or savory

This sauce works well over hearty grains like buckwheat or brown rice. The creamy 'stroganoff' variation works well with egg noodles.

When you make this or any sauce, remember that the intensity of the taste will be diluted by the food you eat it with. So, the sauce by itself should taste strong and rich, too rich to eat by itself, for it to taste good mixed over food. If you season the gravy to taste perfect stand-alone, it will probably taste bland once you pour it over food.

If you use the wine, I suggest an inexpensive hearty red table wine like burgundy. Do not use so-called cooking wine, which is inferior quality and overpriced.

This is a cornstarch gravy, which is textured like sauces you get with Oriental food. It is easy to make and hard to get wrong. Add the cornstarch in small amounts and let it cook in and check the texture, because too much cornstarch will make the gravy almost pudding thick.

3 tbsp peanut or other oil

½ tsp salt ½ tsp black pepper

3 large onions, sliced in crescents

½ tsp or more chopped ginger (optional)

½ tsp sage (optional)

½ tsp thyme (optional) ¼ c wine (optional)

½ tsp rosemary (optional)

2 c water (1 ½ c water if using wine)

1 tbsp cornstarch

2 tbsp miso or to taste

¼ c cold water

Slowly cook the onions and spices (and ginger) in the oil over a low flame until the onions are very soft, the longer the better - at least 15 minutes. Add the water (and wine) and heat slowly, and cook about 5 minutes. Thin the miso with a little bit of the gravy liquid and add it back, and adjust amounts of miso and seasonings. Mix the cornstarch with the cold water and stir into the gravy, and stir until it thickens. If the gravy is still too thin, add a bit more cornstarch and cold water. Adjust salt and pepper one last time if necessary.

Variation: Mushroom 'stroganoff' gravy - Add ½-1 cup chopped mushrooms when the onions are almost done, stir and saute another few minutes .Add 2 tbsp tahini and stir into the sauce when you add the miso to make the sauce creamy. Add 1-2 tbsp red wine vinegar with the tahini to give the gravy a stroganoff type creamy and sour taste.

2021 Update

I was a different person when I first wrote this book back in 2005, and it was a different world. I was cooking for my wife, and my daughter and her friends often joined us. I also cooked for friends quite a bit.

My daughter is now married and has a family of her own, and I live alone. I rarely cook for others, especially since the pandemic and lockdowns have become part of daily life.

My cooking has changed a lot over the years. It has become much simpler and plainer. I use far fewer spices than I used to, and fewer sauces. I still enjoy eating as much as I ever did, but it is now simpler to please my taste.

I am leaving the original spice patterns in the book as-is, partly because the simplifying of my cooking style could be because of my age. I turned 69 this year, and I understand it is typical for older people to come to prefer plainer cooking. That may be the case with me.

The New Edition

I think the main ideas of the book are still just as useful as they were when I wrote the first version of this book over fifteen years ago.

Once you know how to cook a dish with rice, beans and vegetables, you know how to cook dozens and dozens of variants, by varying the type of bean or grain, the type of sauce or no sauce, the combination of spices used, and so on. That is what I am trying to teach in this book.

I still think in terms of basic patterns or templates rather than specific recipes, and I'm surprised that idea hasn't caught on. I suspect most regular cooks operate in those terms whether they realize it or not. Over the years a lot of people have told me they find this book useful, so I'm leaving the core of the book pretty much as-is.

Here I want to talk about the ways I have changed, and what I do differently now. This includes cooking for one, since I have lived alone for the past twelve years.

What is the Same

I still strongly think that imitation meat recipes aren't worth it - they are far too expensive and usually unsatisfying. I still insist you are much better off cooking beans and grains to taste like beans and grains instead of trying to make them act like something else.

I feel the same about all other substitute foods. You will find here no recipes for Vegan Feta or Vegan Steak or Vegan Eggs. Beans taste best when you cook them as beans; rice tastes best when you treat it as rice.

When I want noodles I don't make zucchini noodles or arrowroot noodles or seaweed noodles - I eat noodles.

When I want rice I don't eat cauliflower rice, I eat rice. I love cauliflower, but I love it as cauliflower, not as imitation something else.

Foods high in carbohydrates are now out of style in some circles. When I first learned to cook back in the late 1970's meat and fat were out and brown rice was all the rage. Today, for some types of diet that has flipped; high meat and high fat diets are in and rice and other carbohydrate foods are out.

I can't count the number of times that dietary recommendations have changed just during my lifetime. Fat goes in and out of style; animal fat was out and vegetable oil was in, until vegetable oil became evil and butter came back in style. Meat was out until it was in, at least in some circles. Coconut oil was the worst thing you could eat until it became the healthiest oil to use, and apparently now you again here concerns about it. And so the wheel turns.

I now mostly ignore the changing "scientific" advice and eat what makes me feel good. I pay attention to how food tastes, how I feel when

I am eating and how I feel afterwards. I figured out that I feel bad if I overeat, or if I eat too much fat or sugar. If I eat a lot of one food and start craving a different one I pay attention. I have tried low carbohydrate diets and I find them unsustainable over time. But, if I overeat carbs like overdoing pasta or pancakes I feel bloated, sleepy and spacy.

So, I pay attention. My body gives me the feedback I need.

Differences

These are some of the foods and areas where my opinions have shifted over time.

Mock duck, aka Seitan

I never use it any more. Back in 2005 it was easily available and went for around 55 cents a can if I remember correctly, and a can was good for two meals with my wife and I. As of May 2021 it is now $2.99 a can, which moves it from a staple food to an occasional indulgence.

Chilis

It is obvious to me that I wrote this book while I was first discovering how to cook with different types of chilis. I still love really hot food and eat it a lot, but I now rely more on simple flaked or powdered peppers. I eat a few different kinds of fresh peppers (jalapeno, serrano, and an occasional habanero), and I use dry chipotle for a smoky taste. I most often use an extra hot chili powder I bought at a local Indian grocery, and I keep some ghost pepper flakes around for when I need that over-the-top extra kick.

Spices

I mentioned earlier that I cook with far fewer spices now. Part of that is because spices eventually go stale, and living alone there are only so many spices I can use up before they turn to sawdust. There are now maybe a half dozen spices I use regularly.

If you cook just for yourself, after awhile you will figure out what your favorite spices are, the ones you reach for day after day. It is worth keeping those around, and it is probably not worth buying spices that you use so seldomly that they go stale.

I am also much more prone to cook foods with few or no spices. Rice plus beans is fine with some hot pepper and either soy sauce or fish sauce - maybe a touch of sesame oil if I'm feeling exotic. When I cook with butter or ghee I think foods often taste better with plain salt and pepper.

I now often eat vegetables like broccoli, cauliflower or zucchini steamed and plain, with no seasoning or salt at all. I think they taste a lot better that way.

I really think it is worth cultivating a taste for lightly seasoned or unseasoned foods. It actually ends up expanding the range of tastes you can enjoy.

Variety of beans

I figured out that dry beans have a maximum shelf life of around a year. Past that they take forever to cook or just never get soft. Consequently I buy fewer kinds, especially since I now live alone and cook for one.

I now rely heavily on canned beans. They're cheap, they last forever, and they are very easy to add to a hot dish or salad. Cooking for one, a regular small can of beans is good for two or three days.

Grains

Unlike beans, I have never had a bag of rice go bad on me on the shelf. Regardless of how old the dry rice is it always seems to cook up just fine.

Vinegar

When I was younger I kept around several vinegars - balsamic, rice, wine, apple cider. Now I increasingly just use plain white vinegar. It is easily the cheapest and most widely available. I use vinegar mainly for the sharp sourness, and white vinegar does that as well as any other type. Experiment, and trust your own taste.

Cooking Implements

I still heavily use a pressure cooker and slow cooker. I've never bothered trying an Instant Pot.

I did try out an "Air Fryer" and I think they are over-rated and mis-named. It's a toaster oven with a fan. A convection toaster oven would likely do as well and be more versatile. And no, Air Fryer French Fries don't taste like fries.

I almost never use a regular blender now since cleaning it is a nuisance, but I often use an immersion blender. I never use a food processor for similar reasons. If I want mashed beans for a dip or spread I use a potato masher and the back of a spoon and it's good enough.

I never use a deep fryer. It is just not worth using that much oil all at once with my living alone.

I still use a slow cooker, but I have switched to a smaller one. An inexpensive 2 quart slow cooker is just right for cooking one cup of dry beans - put them in the pot late in the day, turn them on low, and leave them until next morning - 12 to 14 hours without soaking works for the most common beans. It doesn't get any easier than that.

I also use the slow cooker instead of an oven if I want a sweet potato, beet or other root vegetable. It is a way I can oven-cook them without turning on the whole oven.

Buying Organic

I do not worry near as much about buying organic foods as I used to. Unfortunately the word Organic is now very marketable, so organic foods have a hefty markup, often being double the price or more of conventionally grown foods. I figured out I can no longer afford to shop only organic at my local coop - the difference in prices is mind-boggling. I'm disillusioned with the whole organic foods movement which has become an indulgence of the affluent.

Summing Up

I buy simply, I cook simply, I eat simply. I like that.

One Final Secret

This may be the single most important secret to cooking and eating well.

Cook with love and eat with gratitude. The food will be more nourishing and satisfying, and you will be happier.

Giving thanks to God before eating really does make the food taste better, and I think it feeds us at a deeper level. We do not live by bread alone.

May you take the information and techniques in this cookbook and use them to come up with your own style of low budget vegetarian cooking, the style that pleases you and your family the most.

If you are using this cookbook to help take you through challenging financial times, I hope it helps keep you well fed, satisfied and healthy. May God bless and protect you, your friends and family.

About the Author and This Book

Family legend has it that the first thing that Charlie Obert did when he emerged from the womb was to start eating. He has been eating ever since. This first-hand experience of eating is his main qualification to write this book.

Charlie began to cook around the time he realized that he would need to learn to cook in order to continue to eat. So far it seems to be working.

The first edition of this cookbook was written in 2005, when Charlie's daughter Eve was in college. Knowing that she was going to have to learn to cook well in order to avoid being doomed to a lifetime of MacDonald's, Burger King and TV Dinners (anyone remember TV Dinners?), Charlie wrote this book partly as a guide to finding where the real food was hidden in the supermarket in among the fast food, convenience food, junk food, impress-your-neighbors food and Hallmark greeting cards. (Remember, Charlie learned to cook back before Microwave Popcorn had been invented, mostly because Microwave ovens did not yet exist.)

Like the Pearl of Great Price, Charlie figured out that all the finest foods were hidden in the lowliest of places. He is sharing his discovery in this book.

Along with enjoying eating, Charlie also enjoys being able to pay for his food without running up a balance on his credit card.

Fortunately, Charlie never noticed that you are supposed to pay attention to all the latest diets and trends in food, to make sure you are keeping up with your neighbors. This is because he was too busy cooking and eating to notice.

Charlie has never owned a cat. This means that somewhere in the world there is a cat that never had to put up with living with Charlie.

If Charlie had owned a cat it probably would have been named Frank.

Index

CPSIA information can be obtained
at www.ICGtesting.com
Printed in the USA
BVHW050454220921
617191BV00015B/1187